JAVA

The Ultimate Beginner's Guide to Learning Java Programming
Quickly, with No Prior Experience

Mark Reed

Table of Contents

Introduction

Java is a widely used programming language on the Web and in computing applications. It is a free download solution that allows users to access the latest versions and implement updates. This particular programming language is present in the majority of today's web applications and computing technologies. Java's scalable characteristics make it suitable for deployment in a wide range of applications including apps for small electronic devices like cell phones and software solutions for large scale operations such as data centers. The growing preference for deploying Java is attributable to its robust functional features and sound security credentials.

The origin of Java is traceable to 1991 when Sun Microsystems (Sun) unveiled a programming language that was initially known as Oak. The language was developed with the help of five engineers in the company. Interestingly, the Internet was not among the objectives of these engineers when they invented Oak. The team, led by James Gosling, was driven by the primary objective to develop a cross-platform language for the purposes of integrating it into software programs for consumer electronic appliances. The other programming languages at the time, such as C++, were bulky and operated in restricted environments. Oak was meant to introduce the portability, compatibility, and multi-tasking dimensions that would make it possible for the language to be applied in a variety of environments.

Sun introduced further upgrades to Oak and changed the brand name to Java in 1995. The changes marked a dramatic shift that saw the Internet become a core motivation for developing Java. The emergence of the World Wide Web catapulted Java's rise to prominence, thanks to the increased demand for portable and interactive programming languages for the Internet. Oracle assumed the ownership of Java in 2010 when it completed the acquisition of Sun.

This book provides details of the different basic aspects of Java to guide you through the beginner's level of learning the programming language. The book highlights the underlying concepts of Java, provides relevant examples, and incorporates exercises that will help you understand its fundamental parameters, structure, characteristics, and operations. It guides you on the procedures for implementing end-user deployment of the different tools that are used in a Java development environment. Such tools include the Javac compiler for converting source codes into class format, Java Launcher for running Java, and the Javadoc tool for processing and storing documentation. The book also provides tips for deploying applications using the relevant technologies such as the Java Plug-in software solution.

You will find this book useful in understanding the functional aspects of the different toolkits for implementing responsive graphic user interface (GUI) concepts. This includes detailed exploration of the program profile of JavaFX and its relationship to other related GUI solutions such as Swing and Java 3D. The key area of interest in the book will be the libraries and application programming interfaces (APIs) that support the integration of Java applications. APIs are software programs that are designed for use in application development processes. The Java IDL, for example, is equipped with libraries for interacting with remote applications.

Chapter One:
Java Basics

Let us begin by looking at the basic concepts and operations of the Java programming language. Java bears the unique distinction of operating as a modernized programming language but also as a platform. The programming language component of Java is centered on the aspect of writing instructions and compiling commands. The process begins with writing a source code in a plain text file that ends with the *.java* extension. This is followed by the deployment of the Javac compiler that converts the files into *.class* format. The *.class* file hosts bytecodes — that is, the specific language that the Java Virtual Machine (JVM) runs on. The relationship between the JVM and bytecodes is discussed in detail further down the chapter.

The Java platform, on the other hand, is the general environment — be it software or hardware — that hosts program operations. The one outstanding uniqueness of the Java platform is that, unlike other platforms, it strictly operates as software that has capabilities for running on top of other platforms that are hardware-driven. The Java platform comprises the JVM and the Java API for anchoring platform applications and exposing the requisite software development tools, respectively.

Java is present in the software of most of the devices, gadgets, automated systems, and a large variety of information technology equipment that people interact with every other day. Java powers many apps in mobile devices, games, and software programs found in enterprise solutions as well as other types of web content. It could be easily described as the heartbeat of almost all types of network-based applications. Java operates as an object-oriented programming (OOP) platform. This means that Java is written on the basis of standard objects and class parameters.

The convenience of deploying Java lies on its compatibility with most OS platforms including Windows, Mac OS, Linux, and Solaris OS, among others. Java's flexible programmatic features are crucial to the implementation of innovations in the Web and in computing environments. The portability and platform-independence attributes have been the driving force behind its relevance through the years and its growth into a leading programming language. The Java architecture consists of three major components including the Java Development Kit (JDK), the Java Runtime Environment (JRE), and the JVM.

Java Development Kit

The JDK provides the tools needed to build, test, and monitor robust Java-anchored applications. It allows developers to access software components and compile applications during Java programming operations. For example, a developer needs a JDK-powered environment to be able to write applets or implement methods.

Since the JDK more or less performs the operations of a Software Development Kit (SDK), one could easily confuse the scope and operations of the two items. Whereas the JDK is specific to the Java programming language, an SDK has broader applicability. But a JDK still operates as a component of an SDK in a program development environment. This means that a developer would still need an SDK to provide certain tools with broader operational characteristics and that are not available within the JDK domain. Developer documentation and debugging utilities as well as application servers are some of the crucial tools that an SDK supplies to a Java programming environment.

The scope of JDK deployment depends on the nature of the tasks at hand, the supported versions, and the Java edition that is in use. For example, the Java Platform, Standard Edition (Java SE) Development Kit is designed for use with the Java Standard Edition. The Java Platform, Enterprise Edition (Java EE) and the Java Platform, Macro Edition (Java ME) are the other major subsets of the JDK. Details of each of these Java editions are described in detail in the subtopics below. The JDK has been a free platform since 2007 when it was uploaded to the OpenJDK portal. Its open-source status facilitates collaborations and allows communities of software developers to clone, hack, or contribute ideas for advancements and upgrades.

Java SE

The Java SE powers a wide variety of desktop and server applications. It supports the testing and deployment of the Java programming language within the development environment of these applications. Some of the documentations associated with the recent releases of Java SE include an advanced management console feature and a revamped set of Java deployment rules. Java SE 13.0.1 is the latest JDK version for the Java SE platform at the time of writing this book.

The Java SE SDK is equipped with the core JRE capabilities alongside a portfolio of tools, class libraries, and implementation technologies that are designed for use in the development of desktop applications. These tools range from simple objects and types for Java program implementations to advanced class parameters that are suited for building applications with networking capabilities and impenetrable security characteristics. Java programmers can also apply this particular JDK on the development of Java applications used to simplify access to databases or to enhance GUI properties.

Java EE

The Java EE platform is an open-source product that is developed through the collaborative efforts of members of the Java community worldwide. Java EE is closely related to the Java SE because the former is built on top of the latter. This particular software is integrated with transformative innovations that are designed for use in enterprise solutions. The features and advancements that are introduced in new releases often reflect the inputs, requirements, and requests of members of the Java community. The Java EE actually offers more than twenty implementations that are complaint with Java programming.

The Java EE SDK is meant for use in the construction of applications for large-scale operations. Just as its name suggests, this particular Java SDK was created to provide support for enterprise software solutions. The JDK features a powerful API and runtime properties that Java programmers require to build applications with scalable and networkable functionalities. Developers in need of developing multi-tiered applications could find this JDK useful as well.

The Java EE 8 is the latest release at the time of writing this book. Java EE's revised design provides enhanced technologies for enterprise solutions as well as modernized applications for security and management purposes. The release features several advancements that included greater REST API capabilities provided through the Client, JSON Binding, Servlet, and Security APIs. This version also features the Date and Time API as well as the Streams API, according to information published in the Oracle Corporate website as of December 2019.

Java ME

The Java ME platform deploys simplicity, portability, and dynamism to provide a versatile environment for building applications for small gadgets and devices. Java ME is known for having an outstanding application development environment, thanks to its interactive and user-friendly navigation interfaces as well as built-in capabilities for implementing networking concepts. It is largely associated with the Internet of Things (IoT) and is useful when building applications designed for built-in technologies or connected devices that could be used to invent or implement futuristic concepts. Java ME's portability and runtime attributes make it suitable for use in software applications for wearable gadgets, cell phones, cameras, sensors, and printers, among other items and equipment.

The Java ME SDK is equipped with the requisite tools meant for use within an independent environment when developing software applications, testing functionalities, and implementing device simulations. According to information published in the Oracle Corporate website as of 2019, this JDK is well suited for accommodating "the Connected Limited Device Configuration (CLDC)" technology alongside "the Connected Device Configuration (CDC)" functionality. This results in a single and versatile environment for developing applications.

There are several other Java ME solutions that support the deployment of the Java programming language in applications. Java ME Embedded provides a runtime environment integrating IoT capabilities in devices, while the Java ME embedded client facilitates the construction of software solutions that run and optimize the functionality of built-in programs. Java for Mobile makes use of the CLDC and the stack of Java ME developer tools to create innovative features for mobile devices.

Java Runtime Environment

Remember that there are certain conditions that must prevail for Java applications to run efficiently. The JRE contains the ingredients responsible for creating these requisite conditions. This includes the JVM and its corresponding files and class attributes. Although JRE operates as a component of the JDK, it is capable of operating independently, especially if the tasks are limited to run rather than build application instructions.

The JRE lends important operational properties to different programs in the Java programming ecosystem. For example, a program is considered self-contained if it runs an independent JRE within it. This means that a program does not depend on other programs to access to the JRE. This independence makes it possible for a program to achieve compatibility with different OS platforms.

Java Virtual Machine

The JVM operates as a specification for implementing Java in computer programs. It is the driving force behind the platform-independence characteristics of the Java language. This status is accentuated by JVM's status as a program that is executed by other programs. The programs written to interact with and execute the JVM see it as machine. It is for this reason that similar sets, libraries, and interfaces are used to write Java programs to be able to match every single JVM implementation to a particular OS. This facilitates the translation or interpretation of Java programs into runtime instructions in the local OS, and thereby eliminating the need for platform dependence in Java programming.

As a developer you must be wary of the vulnerability your development environment and applications have to cyber attacks and other threats. The JVM provides enhanced security features that protect you from such threats. The solid security foundation is attributable to its built-in syntax and structure limitations that reside in the operational codes of class files. But this does not translate to limitations on the scope of class files that the JVM can accommodate. The JVM actually accepts a variety of class files so long as they can be validated to be safe and secure. Therefore, the JVM is a viable complementary alternative for developing software in other programming languages.

The JVM is often included as a ported feature in a wide variety of software applications and hardware installations. It is implemented through algorithms that are determined by Oracle or any other provider. As such, the JVM provides an open implementation platform. The JVM actually contains the runtime instance as the core property that anchors its command operations. For example, the creation of a JVM instance simply involves writing an instruction in the command prompt that, in turn, runs the class properties of Java.

A Java programmer needs to be familiar with the key areas of JVM such as the classloader and the data section for runtime operations as well as the engine that is responsible for executing programs. There are also performance-related components, such as the garbage collector and the heap dimension tool, that are equally important to the deployment of the JVM. There is a close affiliation between the JVM and bytecodes.

Bytecodes

Bytecodes are essentially JVM commands that are contained in a class file alongside other information that include the symbol table. They operate as background language programs responsible for facilitating the interpretation and execution of JVM operations. Bytecodes are actually the substitutes to native codes because Java does not provide the latter. The structure of the JVM register is such that it contains methods which, in turn, accommodate bytecode streams — that is, sets of instructions for the JVM. In other words, each Java class has methods within it and the class file loading process executes a single bytecode stream for any given method. The activation of a method automatically triggers a bytecode the moment a program begins to run.

The other important feature of bytcodes is the Just-in-time (JIT) compiler that operates during the runtime operations for compiling codes that can be executed. The feature actually exists as a HotSpot JIT compiler within the JVM ecosystem. It executes codes concurrently with the Java runtime operations because it has the ability to perform at optimized levels and the flexibility to scale and accommodate growing traffic of instructions. Previously, the JIT compiler required frequent tuning to rid it of redundant programs and refresh its memory. Tuning was a necessary procedure that ensured the JIT compiler delivered optimum performance. However, the frequent upgrades in the newer versions of Java gradually introduced automated memory refreshing mechanisms that eliminated the need for regular tuning.

Bytecodes can be either primitive types, flexible types, or stack-based. According to Venners (1996), there are seven parameters of primitive data including *byte*, *char*, *double*, *float*, *int*, *long*, and *short*. The *boolean* parameter is also a widely used primitive type, taking the tally to eight. Each of the eight parameters is meant to help developers deploy variables that can be acted upon by the bytecodes. Bytecode streams actually express these parameters of the primitive types in the form of operands. This ends up designating the larger and more powerful parameters to the higher levels of the bytes' hierarchy, with the smaller ones occupying the lower levels of the hierarchy in a descending order.

Java opcodes are similarly crucial components of the primitive types, thanks to their role of classifying operands. This role ensures that operands retain their state, thereby eliminating the need for an operand identification interface in the JVM. The JVM is able to speed up processes because it is capable of multitasking while accommodating multiple opcodes that deliver domicile variables into stacks. Opcodes are also useful for processing and defining the value parameters for stack-based bytecodes. According to Venners (1996), this could be an implicit constant value, an operand value, or a value derived from a constant pool.

The Upsides of Java

- Java epitomizes simplicity in programming, thanks to its user-friendly interface for learning, writing, deployment, and implementation.

- Java's core architecture is designed to facilitate ease of integration and convenience of use within the development environment.

- Java is platform-independent and readily portable, making it suitable for multitasking and use across software applications.

- The object-oriented characteristics of Java support the creation of programs with standard features and codes that can be redeployed.

- Java's networking capabilities make it easier for programmers to create software solutions for shared computing environments.

- The close relationship between Java, the C++, and the C languages makes it easier for anyone with knowledge of the other two languages to learn Java.

- Java's automated garbage collection provides continuous memory protection, making it convenient for programmers to eliminate security vulnerabilities while writing codes.

- Java's architecture is flexible to the implementation of multithreading programs.

- Java is readily reusable, thanks to the ability to redeploy classes using the interface or inheritance features.

The Downsides of Java

- Since Java is not a native application, it runs at lower speeds compared to other programming languages.

- Java may also lack consistency in the processing and displaying of graphics. For example, the ordinary appearance of the graphical user interface (GUI) in Java-based applications is quite different and of lower standards compared the GUI output of native software applications.

- Java's garbage collection, a feature that manages memory efficiency, may interfere with speed and performance whenever it runs as a background application.

JDK Download and Configuration

Most of the widely referenced resources for beginners in Java programming often dive straight into the compiling and running procedures of a Java program. However, one of the major challenges that beginners face is getting lost the moment they are unable to configure Java in the command prompt. In most cases, the command prompt displays error messages indicating the unavailability of the Java program that a newbie is trying to launch. That happens when the path for the Java program has not been set in the command prompt. To avoid such setbacks, perform the initial launch procedures as follows. This guide takes a different approach by beginning from the configuration and launch phase of Java in the command prompt.

- Step one: Download the JDK from the Oracle website and save it in the C drive of your computer. The Oracle download page provides the download links for the latest release and the earlier releases as well as other developer resources for Java programming. This guide is using the jdk-13.0.1 release in Windows 7.

- Step two: Press the Windows and the R keys to launch the pop up window for running programs.

- Step three: Type the phrase cmd.exe in the field and press OK to launch the command prompt.

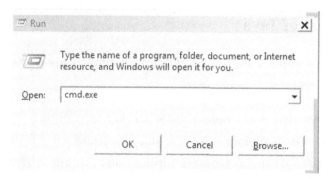

- Step four: Crosscheck the command prompt window that pops up to ensure that it contains the relevant descriptions. The users name will depend on the one set in your computer.

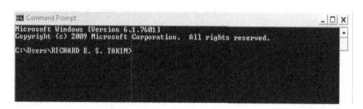

- Step five: Enter these particulars — Set path= — right after the > sign (do not enter space in between). Locate the folder where you saved the JDK download and copy the path of the JDK. The file path for this guide was C:\Program Files\Java\jdk-13.0.1\bin. Paste the path right after the = sign and press Enter. This procedure sets the path for your JDK as follows:

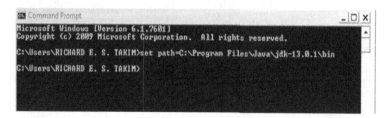

You can be sure at this point that your JDK is properly downloaded and configured in the system. You can now proceed to the next phase of writing your first Java program. However, the above procedure is a temporary solution because you will have to set the path every time you launch the command prompt. It is worth understanding it as a beginner because it could be helpful in the initialization of your Java programs. The exercise at the end of this chapter will guide you on how to permanently set the path.

Compile and Run the First Java Program

The compilation of the first Java programs for beginners often revolves around the "Hello World" and "My First Java Program" phrases. That does not mean that those are the only phrases that you can use to compile your programs. You can use any names as long as you get the coding right and save your files in the recommended format. The preferred phrase for this guide is "My Simple Java Program". You need a text editor, preferably Notepad, to be able to compile your first Java program.

- Step one: Create and name a folder in your preferred location. This folder will provide storage for both your Notepad document and the class file that will be created. For purposes of simplicity, this guide has named the folder MySimpleJavaProgram.

- Step two: Open Notepad and type the following instructions.

- Step three: Save the file in the destination folder. Remember the file name must be saved in a .java format. For example, the file name for this guide would be MyFirstJavaProgram.java. Change the file type from Text Document to All Files.

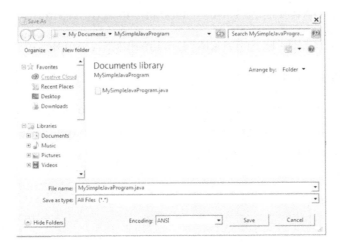

- Step four: Open a command prompt and change the file path to match the path of the compiled Java program in the destination folder. Looking at the example in this guide, the MySimpleJavaProgram.java folder is stored in Documents in the MySimpleJavaProgram folder. Therefore, the initial step here would be to change the directory to Documents by typing >cd documents and pressing Enter.

Microsoft Windows [Version 6.1.7601]

Copyright (c) 2009 Microsoft Corporation. All rights reserved.

C:\Users\RICHARD E. S. TAKIM>cd documents

- Step five: Type >cd MySimpleJavaProgram to change the directory to the destination folder and press Enter.

Microsoft Windows [Version 6.1.7601]

Copyright (c) 2009 Microsoft Corporation. All rights reserved.

C:\Users\RICHARD E. S. TAKIM>cd documents

C:\Users\RICHARD E. S. TAKIM\Documents>cd MySimpleJavaProgram

- Step six: Proceed to type >javac MySimpleJavaProgram.java and press Enter to compile the program.

Microsoft Windows [Version 6.1.7601]

Copyright (c) 2009 Microsoft Corporation. All rights reserved.

C:\Users\RICHARD E. S. TAKIM>cd documents

C:\Users\RICHARD E. S. TAKIM\Documents>cd MySimpleJavaProgram

C:\Users\RICHARD E. S. TAKIM\Documents\MySimpleJavaProgram>javac

MySimpleJavaProgram.java

- Step seven: If successful, the procedures above will result in a command prompt window that resembles the one below. The procedure will effectively have created a class file of the program.

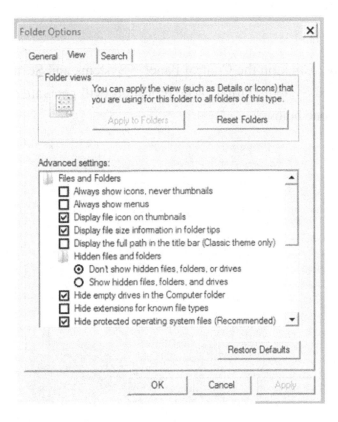

Important Program Compilation Tips

In step two, although many resources have the second and third lines indented, such indentation does not affect the processing of the coding when using the command prompt. In some cases, the indentation usually occurs as a default feature in some integrated development environments (IDEs).

In step three, there are occasions when the .txt extension could remain hidden and attached on a saved file name as .java.txt. Such a mishap would mean that the command prompt would not be able to trace the file response when you finally run the javac program. To avoid the .txt format, click Computer > Organize > Folder and Search Options > View. Uncheck the "Hide extensions for known file types" as demonstrated below.

In step four, you could experience trouble locating your file or having the command prompt generating warnings that a file cannot be found or recognized. To solve such problems, you would need to confirm whether or not the file has been loaded into the command prompt directory. Open the command prompt and change directory to the location of your program's destination folder, press Enter and type DIR. For example type >cd Documents, press Enter and then type >DIR. Scan through the results to find out if the destination folder or the program file is loaded. For example, the results below show that the MySimpleJavaProgram is available in the directory.

```
06/25/2019  05:13 PM    <DIR>         Fax
01/10/2020  07:23 PM    <DIR>         Java Programs
03/01/2016  05:23 PM    <DIR>         My ISO Files
01/05/2020  08:54 PM    <DIR>         MySimpleJavaProgram
04/30/2018  10:12 AM    <DIR>         OneNote Notebooks
09/16/2019  08:01 AM    <DIR>         Scanned Documents
```

Exercise

Use the systems portal in your Windows program to set a permanent path for your Java program and test the path in the command prompt. Explain each of the steps that you performed.

Solution:

- Step one: Click on the Control Panel > Systems and Security > Systems > Advanced System Settings. The procedure will generate a pop-up window like the one below.

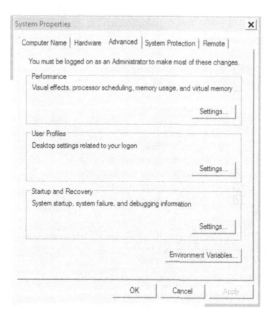

- Step two: Click on the Environment Variables tab to proceed to a window that resembles the one below.

- Step three: Click on the new tab under the system variables section. Type JAVA_HOME in the variable name field and copy/paste the storage path to your JDK download in the variable value field. Ideally, this would be C:\Program Files\Java\jdk-13.0.1\bin; and it is important to include the semicolon at the end of the path to avoid error setbacks in your upcoming command prompt operations. Click OK to save the changes and close the window.

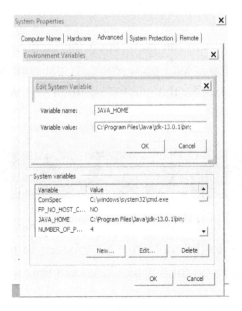

- Step four: Click on the new tab under the system variables section again. Type the word Path in the variable name field and copy/paste the storage plus the bin path — that is,

C:\Program Files\Java\jdk-13.0.1\bin; %JAVA_HOME%\bin; — to your JDK download in the variable value field. Click OK to save the changes and close the window.

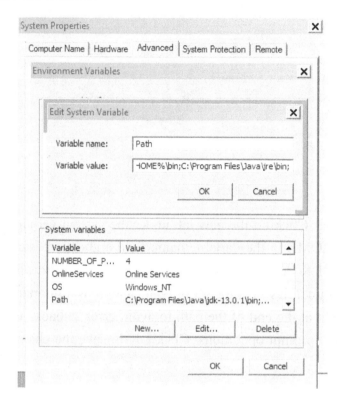

- Step five: To confirm the path, open the command prompt and type the words *javac –version* and press enter. If the command prompt displays a message that looks like the one below, then you will have successfully set the permanent path.

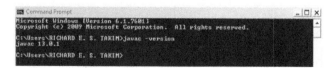

Step six: To find out all the details of the Java you have installed, type >cd C:\\ to change the directory to the root drive C. Proceed to type *>java –version* and press Enter. The Java version for this particular example appeared as follows.

17

Chapter Summary

- The JDK, the JRE, and the JVM are the three major components of the architecture of the Java programming language.

- Java programming uses bytecodes to process application building processes because it is not equipped with native codes.

- Java must be configured appropriately after installation for the developer to be able to compile and run programs.

In the next chapter you will learn about the basic structure of a Java program.

Chapter Two:
Program Profile and Structure

To help you understand how the Java language works, this chapter explores each of the basic components of the program's structure. The Java program structure is the basic procedure for writing or formatting programs in Java language. It is actually the manner in which a Java program is written.

Although the widely recommended Java program structure may vary to some degree among different Java resources, a majority of the resources suggest a structure consisting of six sections. The variations are minor as they concern the sequence or the naming of the sections. But there is overwhelming consensus among these resources about the underlying concepts and principles of the sections and their significance to the overall program structure in Java. The sections include documentation, class definition, and main method as well as package, import, and interface statements.

Recommended
Documentation or Comment Section
Optional
Package Statement Import Declaration Interface Statement
Compulsory
Class Definition Main Method Definition

The method declaration and the class definition are the only essential sections of a program structure. The documentation section is recommended while the rest are optional. Whereas the essential section is mandatory and generates error warnings if left out, the optional sections do not cause errors if you choose to exclude them.

Documentation or Comment Section

You would ideally use the documentation section as a guide on the different coding aspects of the Java program. Comments describe the useful methods, operations, or variables for implementing or debugging program codes. Such comments can also be used to hide the program codes, albeit temporarily. The one outstanding aspect of the comments feature is its flexibility to fit in any part of the code. This is because the compiler and the interpreter leave out the comments when executing Java programs, considering that their roles are restricted to enhancing readability.

The Java programming language provides support for single line, multiline, and documentation comments. Just as the name suggests, a single line comment occupies one line of coding. It begins with a double forward slash followed by the comment. The declaration does not require a closing symbol at the end.

// this is a declaration for the single-line comment

The multiline comment occupies several lines of the code. It begins with a single forward slash followed by an asterisk. The declaration must be closed with an asterisk followed by a forward slash. In other words, the forward slash encloses all the contents of the multiline comment.

/* this is a declaration for the multiline comment that runs two lines and is appropriately enclosed by the forward slash */

As for the documentation comment, it stretches over the entire code. The documentation comment is designed for use in the Javadoc tool when creating API documentations. It begins with a single forward slash followed by double asterisk. The declaration must be closed with a single asterisk followed by a forward slash. Just like the multiline comment, the forward slash encloses all the contents of the document comment.

/** this is a declaration for the document comment and it can run several lines to form a block before it is closed at the end with the relevant symbol */

Package Statement

The package statement section provides room for bundling and declaring classes. This way, a namespace can be used to indicate the storage destination of the classes. The package statement is useful in creating class categories on the basis of their functions because a Java program accommodates only a single package statement at any given time. Package declaration must be positioned at the head of the code prior to class or interface declarations. The package statement can be generated using any name as long as it is representative of the classes that are declared within it. The example below shows the simple profile of a package statement.

package trainers;

The declaration made by this particular statement recognizes all the class and interface definitions of the source file as segments of the trainers package. Each source file contains only a single source package. Since the package statement is one of the optional sections of a program structure, it provides mechanisms for transforming the class names into a default package in the event that a programmer chooses to leave it out.

Import Declaration

An import declaration is a description of the composition of packages. This section actually shows the details of the classes that are contained within the storage domain of other packages. The import declaration statement comes in handy when a developer needs access to particular classes that are within other packages. A simple importation of the target package into a program would do the trick. Import declaration is an optional section that is inserted right next to the package statement. There is the flexibility of importing as many classes as possible into a single program. A Java programmer can generate several import declarations when writing programs, as demonstrated by the two examples below.

1 import java.io*;

2 import java.applet.*;

The file import statement imports a specified class of a Java program, while the second statement triggers the importation of the entire class definitions contained in the Java Applet. That is the reason why import statements precede class definitions, because they give instructions on the actions to be performed in the classes.

Interface Statement

An interface is the point of separation between systems but also the conveyor of data communications between the systems. In Java programming, an interface is an agent for implementing abstraction, in that it is useful for managing complexities in coding and enhancing readability. The interface statement section of a Java program houses instructions such as methods and constants, which are useful in the achievement of object inheritance implementations. This section is similarly optional and it provides room for the implementation of multiple inheritances during programming.

interface stack{

The interface statement begins with a simple statement that is closed at the end by a curly brace. Since the interface is not flexible to instantiation, the properties of its operations can be stretched using class definitions. The use of multiple interfaces can also be used to compensate the lack of instantiation mechanisms in the interface.

Class Definition

A class is a critical component of Java programming that contains assorted variables and methods required to sustain operations in program fields. The class definition section provides descriptions of the different classes within a program. Every Java program is equipped with a minimum of one class alongside the declaration for the main method. There are no limitations as to the maximum number of classes that can be contained in a program. When writing a program, it is important to assign names to the classes hosted in Java files. The names will be needed during the creation of objects of the classes within other programs.

Main Method

The main method describes the runtime properties of the Java program. It is actually the launching pad for applications in the JRE. As such, the main method is the ignition point for executing Java applications. It accommodates a single class at any given time, despite the availability of multiple classes within the Java program structure. The main method carries the declarations for data types and prescribes the sequence for executing statements. Let's refer to the first Java program that we compiled, the MySimpleJavaProgram, to dissect the main method declaration and its underlying operations.

```
public class MySimpleJavaProgram{

public static void main(String args[]){

System.out.println("My Simple Java Program File");

}

}
```

The first line of the program is a class declaration, while the second line is a main method declaration. A program's core instruction that facilitates its execution is housed in the main method. Every item in the main method plays a specific role. For example, the Public keyword makes the main method available or accessible to other program parameters. Although the Static keyword would be optional to developers, it still provides important definitions for executing the program. It actually signals the accessibility of a method despite the absence of its object definitions. The Void expression signals to the computer that the program is not expected to generate anything at that particular point of the instruction. The Main keyword is the actual method and it is recognized as the essential segment of the Java program.

The curly braces show a program's start and end points, while the brackets describe a method's expected inputs. Since the [] parameters represent arrays, the expected input of this particular program is a String of instructions that are predefined by the args or arguments. The System.out.println instruction in line three is responsible for delivering the phrase "My Simple Java Program File" to the program for execution by the computer. This means that the computer takes over to execute the commands and generate the specified output from the program's instructions.

Exercise

Compile and run a Java program that has a document/comment section, a class definition, main method and at least one of the optional statements – that is, a package, an import, or an interface statement.

Solution:

package trainers;

public class TrainingManual{

/* trainer qualifications

* college degree

*professional experience

*/

public static void main(String[] args){

//comment: output requirements specified

System.out.println("Training Manual and Trainer Requirements");

}

}

The solution above compiles and runs successfully because it has a package statement, a class definition, a multi line document/comment section, a single-line comment, and a main method definition.

Chapter Summary

- Although the Java program structure has six different components, the method declaration and the class definition are the only essential sections.

- The class definition section contains detailed descriptions of the different classes within a program.

- The main method declaration is useful for launching the operations of applications in the JRE.

In the next chapter you will learn about the profile and primary characteristics of a data program in Java.

Chapter Three:
Data Profile and Structure

Speed and efficiency are the primary motivations behind the design of data structure in Java. The Java data structure supports the storage and manipulation of data in computers, servers, or any other networked devices. Efficiency and operational scopes of the data structure dictate the design of algorithms. These algorithms are actually the specific procedures or instructions that signal and prompt computers to perform complex tasks. Data structures operate as built-in installations in the Java API. There are different types of data structures including arrays, hashtable, linked list, searching, stack, queue, and vector, among others. This chapter focuses on a couple of the data structures that are relevant to your level as a Java beginner.

Arrays

Just like the rest of the subsets of the Java data structure, the array is a built-in functionality. The syntax feature in Java language helps trigger and define array declarations. This makes it easier for a Java programmer to build a non-primitive type array. Notably, certain conditions must prevail in the Java development environment for the array to operate efficiently. The array can only accommodate similar object types due to its homogeneity attributes. For example, a developer cannot store a String once an Integer in is stored in an *int []* already. A String can only be accepted by a *String []* array. Such an attempt would generate an error message during runtime operations. Moreover, the indices in use must be valid to avoid error messages because array operations in Java programming are bounded.

Data type and array name are the core components of an array declaration. Simply expressed as *data type[] arrayName*, the data type bit describes the primitive or non-primitive properties of the data while the arrayName is an identification parameter. An array expressed using the primitive data type *int[] units;* would have the units bit as the identifier. This structure in itself shows that the units section is the array responsible for housing the values of the data type int.

The array is designed to accommodate a single element or multiple elements. For an array to accommodate a single element, it would be expressed as follows:

int[] units;

units = new int[];

The data types can always change depending on the nature of the arrays that you are processing. For the code above to accommodate multiple elements, the number of elements must be specified as demonstrated in the example below.

int[] units;

units = new int[4];

The insertion of the digit signals that the array has been set to accommodate four elements. An array declaration does not necessarily have to occupy multiple lines; an operator such as the equal sign can be used to transform the two lines into a single line declaration. For example, the declaration the primitive data type 'char' and its 'units' identifier in the earlier examples can be transformed as follows.

int[] units = new int[4];

The connection of the two lines has simply involved the removal of the semicolon symbol at the end of the identifier and the deletion of one of the identifiers. The significance of a single line declaration structure lies in the fact that it simplifies the dissection of the different components of an array index in Java. Indices are very important components of arrays in Java programming because they dictate the speeds of operations in the arrays. The index actually hosts the data structure of the array, meaning that its overall design determines the output of the array. Factors such as the number of elements in an array along with its length determine the composition of the code. An ideal array would appear like the one below that has been created using an int[] scores = new int[4]; declaration.

introductory element	score[0]	score[1]	score[2]	score[3]	
					final element
index bar	0	1	2	3	

An interpretation of the above illustration of an array structure shows that it has got a length of four elements. The pattern of the element is such that the score value matches a corresponding index value. For example, the introductory element

26

has a [0] score and corresponding zero index. However, there is clear disparity between the score and index of the last element on the one hand and the total number of elements. For this case the corresponding value of score and index of the final element is [3] and 3, respectively, while the length of elements is 4. The disparity arises because array always has a default initial value that is usually a zero for numeric elements or false for non-numeric elements. It is for this reason that an array's length is expressed as n, so that the final element can be expressed as n-1. This means the final element of an array will always be less than that of the total number of elements by a single digit.

The declaration procedure also permits the concurrent initialization of the array. This affords you the flexibility of either initializing during the declaration phase, or keeping the initialization exercise pending until the later stages of program compilation. But rather than having the square brackets around the values, declaration-time initialization deploys the curly braces.

```
int[] scores = {68, 80, 74, 86};
```

The sequence of this particular declaration-time initialization shows that the values of the elements do not follow any particular pattern. Basically, its position of the element value is dictated by the array declaration. However, the array declaration and the indices must follow corresponding patterns and bear corresponding values as well.

By this point, you have all the ingredients that you would require to code an array, including the indices, the declaration, and the initialization properties. You can use this information to compile and run a code that will generate your desired output. If we were to use the properties and values of the illustration of the array structure, we will end up with the code below.

```
class CompileArray{

public static void main(String[] args){

int[] score = new int[4];

System.out.println(score[0]);

System.out.println(score[1]);

System.out.println(score[2]);
```

```
System.out.println(score[3]);

    }

}
```

When you run this program, it will return 0 values for all the four fields because the illustration did not specify values for the elements. The outcome underscores the direct relationship between the indices and the elements of an array.

LinkedList

The LinkedList provides a mechanism for processing data in a predefined or controlled sequence. It operates as a component of the larger collection framework in Java. As such, the LinkedList contains the properties required to manipulate the interface for collections and iterations. This includes the Java List, the Java queue, and the Java deque interfaces. These interfaces form a tree-like structure with the collection framework sitting at the top, and the list and the queue sitting side-by-side below it. The deque is more or less a subset of the queue, and is part of the chain of inheritance that runs right to the collection framework. In other words, the queue interface extends the properties of the collection framework, while the deque extends the properties of the queue in the implementation of the LinkedList.

The double nature of the LinkedList is attributed to a node list that provides support for three core paths, namely the previous, data, and next. A node list is basically an element of a LinkedList. The 'previous' segment is denoted as 'prev.' and it contains the address particulars of the list's preceding element. The address particulars of the succeeding element are housed in the 'next' segment. Both the prev. and next field have null values for their introductory elements. As for the data segment of the node, it is the storage destination of the information generated by the node.

The storage of elements in an overlapping format rather than a hierarchy structure is the other notable characteristic of the LinkedList. The Prev. and Next addresses of the node are used to establish connectivity between the elements. Let us use Bentley, Ford, and Toyota as the three data segments of the node. The first introductory element would have a null value in Prev., followed by Bentley and next. The second element would have Prev., Ford, and next. In this case, the Prev.

address in the Ford element will be connected back to Bentley, while the next address in the Bentely element will be connected to the Ford data segment. Similar connection procedures will occur in the Prev. and next addresses of Ford and Toyota. But since Toyota is the final element, it will have a null value to close the process of linking the list.

The creation of a LinkedList code in Java is often guided by the description of its type. This could be an integer, double, short, long, or string type. Interfaces and methods provide accessibility definitions to the LinkedList code. For example, accessibility to methods contained in a declared linked list is restricted to the corresponding interface. This means that a declared LinkedList of the Queue interface can only access the method in the queue interface and not deque interface, and vice versa. Examine the code below to gauge your understanding of the different aspects of the structure of a LinkedList.

```
import java.util.LinkedList;

public class MainScores {

public static void main(String[] args){

LinkedList<String> scores = new LinkedList<>();

// Add elements to LinkedList

scores.add("10");

scores.add("20");

scores.add("30");

System.out.println("LinkedList: " + scores);

}

}
```

The output for this particular code is: [10, 20, 30]. This example uses the add() method approach to inserting elements to the LinkedList. The addition of the scores has been defined by the single-line declaration comment. There are several other methods for inserting elements into a LinkedList, including the get() method and Iterator() method. LinkedList also features procedures for searching, changing, and removing elements. You will learn more about these methods and approaches gradually as you get used to the coding conventions of Java programming.

LinkedList versus ArrayList

Java's ArrayList feature helps build unique collection objects. Although closely related to the array, the ArrayList bears functionality attributes that are designed to overcome the challenges of array operations. For example, the array list has automated resizing capabilities, allows deletions, and accommodates additional parameters within the body of the collection.

Comparisons between the LinkedList and the ArrayList show that both are useful in the creation of the list interface. However, there are significant differences in their internal structures and operations that would make one preferable over the other in coding implementations. For example, the manipulation of the array size is the underlying operational procedure of the ArrayList. The LinkedList does not offer such flexibility in its operational procedure because it is tied to its own replication. The other differences between the ArrayList and LinkedList include:

- ArrayList operates at faster speeds than the LinkedList because its data structure is anchored on the index. This structure makes it easier for the ArrayList to exploit the getIndex() properties of arrays, with the only requirement being that all the acquired elements always have to be rearranged. The LinkedList is not equipped with the index-compatible paths for accessing data and the developer must initiate the commands for retrieving the data.

- LinkedList has an edge over the ArrayList when it comes to procedures for inserting data or any other operations parameters. This is because the LinkedList does not require resizing manipulations, especially when there is need to add it to a newly created array in case a destination array is filled up. The ArrayList requires resizing and reconfiguration of the index to reflect updates when any insertions are made to the code.

- The procedure for removing data or other operation parameters is much easier in the LinkedList relative to the same procedure in the ArrayList.

- The LinkedList utilizes more memory because it concurrently accommodates data and other descriptive details, such as addresses, within the node. This is unlike the ArrayList which rationalizes its memory use through the hosting of actual objects in indices.

Notably, developers generally prioritize the ArrayList over the LinkedList despite the latter's accommodative structure to insertions and removals compared to the former. The preference for the ArrayList is associated with its wider scope of application compared to the LinkedList.

Stack

The stack component of the data structure operates in a last in, first out (LIFO) format. This simply means that the latest element to be added to the stack would be lined up for consumption before the rest. This sequence is replicated throughout the process such that the oldest elements to be added would only be consumed if no new elements are added on the stack. It is for this reason that the stack component of the data structure features both the push and pop methods. Whereas the push parameter is ideal for inserting objects, the pop property provides the mechanisms for detecting, selecting, and removing the latest additions to a stack. These functions of the stack are in contrast to the stack memory, which is primarily used for storage of various components of Java such as methods. Therefore, the two cannot be substituted for each other. The example below shows how to write a Stack code using the push method.

```
import java.util.Stack;

public class Main{

public static void main(String[] args){

Stack <Integer> scores = new Stack<>();

//Add the following items to Stack

scores.push(1);

scores.push(2);

scores.push(3);

System.out.println("Stack: " + scores);

}
```

}

This particular example used the integer type to generate the result, Stack: [1,2,3]. You could alternatively use the String type or any other type, but you must change all the other parameters to comply with the coding of your chosen type.

Hashtable

The hashtable, also known as the dictionary, contains the ingredients for manipulating and aligning data on the basis of predefined properties. It actually gives users the flexibility for defining the core aspects of the data structure. For example, a location-based parameter, such as longitude and latitude position, could be used as a substitute for the name of a hospital. The Hashtable is subject to interpretation because the meaning assigned to the core aspects of the structure is determined by its deployment.

Hashtable is alternatively referred to as a map data structure because it is endowed with rich features for assigning keys to values. It only needs any key, as long as it is not null, to utilize the prescribed functionality for mapping values. The Hashtable has within it the 'Properties' subset that is useful for capturing String parameters of value listings.

```
import java.util.Hashtable;

public class TableHash {

public static void main(String[] args){

Hashtable<String, Integer> scores = new Hashtable<String, Integer>();

//put scores to Hashtable

  scores.put("one", 1);

  scores.put("two", 2);

  scores.put("three", 3);

  System.out.println("Hashtable: = " + scores);

}

}
```

The code should generate the outcome, Hashtable: = {two=2, one=1, three=3}.

The combination of the String and the Integer in the interface statement is the conspicuous feature of this particular coding. Moreover, the scores represent the keys required to map target values. This shows that the Hashtable provides room for operational modification once the iterator has been put in place.

Queue

The queue is essentially a linear structure that organizes data in a first in, first out (FIFO) format. This way, elements in a collection are arranged in a specified order that facilitates exit and entry operations at the head and the tail, respectively. Head operations involving the exit of data are known as 'dequeue', while tail end operations involving the entry of data is called 'enqueue' (Gootooru, 2019). The dequeuing and enqueuing operations occur upon the return of the values for the head and tail operations, respectively. The sequence of exit and entry events in the queue data structure is the direct opposite of stack's LIFO format, since the oldest elements exit first to create room for new elements

```java
import java.util.LinkedList;

import java.util.Queue;

public class TestCode{

public static void main(String[] args){

Queue<Integer> t = new LinkedList<>();

t.add(11);

t.add(23);

t.add(31);

System.out.println("the created queue is: " + t);

int num0 = t.remove();

System.out.println("the item removed from the queue is: " + num0);

System.out.println("state of the queue after removal is: " + t);

int first = t.peek();

System.out.println("the new item at the beginning of the queue is: " + first);

}
```

}

Since the code is designed to consume the oldest items to create room for news one, it will display the results below. If you scrutinize the code, the result shows that the developer can manipulate the number and size of items in the fields, but not the order of the exit of the items. The head item must be the first one to exit.

The created queue is: [11, 23, 31]

The item removed from the queue is: 11

State of the queue after removal is: [23, 31]

The new item at the beginning of the queue is: 23

Exercise

Use the following declaration-time array initialization — int[] scores = {68, 80, 74, 86}; — to compile and run a code using array values [0] to [3] and indices 0 to 3 on an array that is 4 elements long.

Solution:

The diagram below represents the array structure with the first row representing the array declaration, the second row representing the elements, and the third row representing the indices.

score[0]	score[1]	score[2]	score[3]
68	80	74	86
0	1	2	3

The code for the above array would have values for the elements, unlike the array structure illustration that was used to code the array in the previous example.

class ArrayScore {

public static void main(String[] args) {

int[] score = new int[4];

//enter 68 to introductory element

score[0] = 68;

//enter 80 to element two

```java
score[1] = 80;

//enter 74 to element three

score[2] = 74;

//enter 86 to final element

score[3] = 86;

for (int i = 0; i < 4; ++i) {

System.out.println("element and corresponding index" +": " + score[i]);

}

}

}
```

The above program will generate the output below:

element and corresponding index 0: 68

element and corresponding index 1: 80

element and corresponding index 2: 74

element and corresponding index 3: 86

However, a casual scrutiny over the code reveals some differences with the previous coding structures. For example, unlike the previous coding structures that end with two curly braces at the bottom, this particular code has three curly braces. There are several other differences that have been occasioned by the use of the looping construction method that is widely known as 'for loop' in computer programming circles. You will encounter more details concerning the 'for loop' construction at the intermediate level of Java programming.

Chapter Summary

- There is close relationship between the data structure and the design and efficiency of algorithms.

- The homogeneity attributes of the array restricts its compatibility to similar object types.

- The LinkedList is one of the crucial components of the data structure in

Java because it contains the properties required to manipulate the interface for collections and iterations.

In the next chapter you will learn about the roles of variables and data types in Java programming.

Chapter Four:
Variables and Data Types

Now that we have learned to compile and run the Java program in addition to studying its structure, let's train our focus on the variables and data types of the program. This chapter is going to help you understand the core elements of a Java program and the procedure for declaring those elements.

Java programs consist of various parameters that facilitate their operations and implementations. Variables, data types, and operators are the core elements of the functional infrastructure of the Java programs. A variable houses the values of a Java program, while a data type is the corresponding parameter that defines the qualitative and quantitative properties of the values in each variable. Operators, on the other hand, are simply the command functionalities that facilitate the controlled manipulation of variables. An understanding of the structures and operations of each of these parameters will be helpful in learning the Java basics or advancing Java skills.

The deployment of a variable is a procedural experience that involves declaring the characteristics of the variable and initializing its value. The declaration phase requires one to provide a specific description for the data type and assign a unique identity to the variable. The initialization phase reveals the exact value of a variable. Once a variable has been declared and initialized, the two segments can be combined to generate executable instructions. For example, if the data type, the variable name, and the variable value are char, count, and 20, respectively, then the combination would be: char count = 20. Moreover, an initialized variable must be assigned a value for it to compile successfully. Assignment involves substituting the default value of an initialized variable with an executable value. To understand the significance of initialization, open a Notepad, type the instructions, save the file as InitializeProgram.java, and run the program in Java.

```
public class InitializeProgram{

public static void main(String[] args)

{

int i;
```

System.out.println("i is" + i);

}

}

The program did not compile and instead generated the error message below:

InitializeProgram.java:5: error: variable i might not have been initialized

System.out.println("i is" + i);   ^

1 error

The above error occurred because the computer did not recognize the 'i' symbol after the + operator in line four. The default variable must be assigned a value for it to be initialized during compilation. This is achieved by simply substituting the 'i' symbol after the + operator with either a numeric or qualitative value. Open the InitilizeProgram.java Notepad file that you used in the above example and edit it to appear like the one below. This program will successfully compile and run to create a class file because the variable has been initialized by an appropriate assignment statement right after the int i; declaration and right before the System.out.println method. Moreover, the 'i' symbol after the + operator has been replaced with a value of 3. As such, variables are initialized through the coding of assignment statements.

public class InitializeProgram{

public static void main(String[] args)

{

int i;

i = 3;

System.out.println("i is" + 3);

}

}

Types of Variables

A variable may be local, instance, or static. The type of variable depends on the nature of its declaration, assignment, or initialization.

Local Variable

The declaration of a local variable takes place within a method's body. The declaration operation is restricted within the method, such that other methods within a particular class category remain unaware of the existence of the variable. However, it is possible to declare a local variable with a similar variable identification or name in several methods. One other outstanding feature of a local variable is that it is not allocated an initial value by default. The value must be initialized, or else the compiler will always generate an error message as seen in the examples above. Follow the steps below to compile and run a sample program with the age and player name as your local variables defining hockey and coach profiles.

Step One: Open your text editor and type this code.

```
public class HockeyTeam{

public void Hockey()

{

//local variable age

//local variable player

int age = 18;

String player = "John";

age = age + 2;

System.out.println("Hockey player is: " + player + " player age is: " + age);

player = "Mike";

System.out.println("Hockey player is: " + player + " player age is: " + age);

}

public void CoachProfiles()

{

int age = 35;

String coach = "John";
```

```
age = age + 4;

System.out.println("Hockey coach is: " + coach + " coach name is: " + age);

coach = "Susan";

System.out.println("Hockey coach is: " + coach + " coach name is: " + age);

}

public static void main(String args[])

{

HockeyTeam hoc = new HockeyTeam();

}

}
```

Step two: Compile and run the code in a command prompt or IDE to generate a result like the one below.

Player name is: John

Player age is: 18

Player name is: Mike

Player age is: 20

Coach name is: John

Coach age is: 35

Coach name is: Susan

Coach age is: 39

This outcome demonstrates that any given local variable can be assigned by declaring similar names, in this case age and player, in two separate methods — that is, Hockey and CoachProfiles.

Instance Variable

As for an instance variable, the declaration operation is exterior to the method but interior to the class category. This means that other methods are aware of the existence of the variable. However, the value of this particular type of variable is specific to the corresponding instances within a class. There are no permissible paths for sharing values across instances located in different classes. An instance variable does not have to be initialized because it has a default zero, false, or null values depending on the nature of data type. The example below demonstrates the procedure for implementing multiple object declarations for instance variables.

```java
import java.io.*;

class Cars{

//q is an instance variable

//q variable declaration is occurring within a class rather than method

int q;

}

public class CarUnits{

public static void main(String args[])

{

//object 1 declaration

Object obj1 = new Object();

int q = 8;

//Object 2 declaration

Object obj2 = new Object();

int r = 5;

//value displays for object 1

System.out.println("object 1 values");

System.out.println(obj1);

//value displays for object 2

System.out.println("Object 2 values");

System.out.println(obj2);

}
```

}

This example has declared two different instance variables q and r in two different objects 1 and 2. The output of the program will designate value 8 to the first object and value 5 to the second object. It is evidence of the non-static properties of the instance variable that accommodate the allocation of memory to variables upon the construction of new objects.

Static Variable

A static variable, on the other hand, is readily shared among different instances within a class. Its declaration occurs right at the program's head where it is followed by the keyword. Just like an instance variable, initialization in a static variable is not compulsory because it features a default zero value. However, unlike an instance variable, a static variable does not allow the construction of new objects to trigger the allocation of memory for variables. This is because the memory allocation is strictly a one-time process that happens during the loading phase of the class. Moreover, whereas an instance variable restricts the reflection of a change of value within an object, a static variable reflects the changes made to a particular object on other multiple objects. Use the example given below as a guide to compile a static variable and understand the different parameters of its operation structure.

```
public class StaticVariable{

static String base=("start");

public void creation()

{

//base

}

public static void main(String args[])

{

StaticVariable lan1=new StaticVariable();

StaticVariable lan2=new StaticVariable();

lan1.creation();
```

```
lan2.creation();

System.out.println("lan1: base is="+lan1.base);

System.out.println("lan2: base is="+lan2.base);

}

}
```

The outcome of the code is:

lan1: base is=start

lan2: base is=start

Primitive Data Types

Java data types are classified into primitive data types and non-primitive data types. The primitive category refers to data types that have been defined in advance with the Java programs. There are eight primitive data types, and they are already mentioned in Chapter One under the Bytecodes subheading. This section will explore the scope and function of each of these data types. Some of the eight primitive data are number types that are further split into integer or floating point types. Integer data types exist as numeric values that are stored as whole numbers. The *byte*, *int*, *long*, and *short* parameters fall within this particular subcategory. Floating point data types are numeric values with fractions and it mainly consists of the *double* and *float* parameters. The *char* and the *boolean* data types are independent of the two subcategories.

The *byte* type is designed for the storage of non-fraction numbers with values ranging from -128 to 127. It is particularly useful in situations where programmers seek to minimize memory use. The *short* type provides a wider range of values running to tens of thousands, making it suitable for small- to medium-scale data storage. The *int* type is suited for large scale data storage as it accommodates whole numbers within the range of over negative 2 billion to 2 billion. This particular data type is suited for situations that require numeric values when generating variables. The *long* type provides the widest range of data storage spanning over tens of quintillions.

The *float* data type is meant for use in storing numbers that have decimal points. The letter "f" is used at the end to specify the float status of numeric values. The *double* type is similar to the *float* type with the exception of its wide range of data storage. It requires the use of a "d" at the end as well to specify the *double* status of values. The *double* type is capable of accommodating up to 15-digit decimal points while the *float* type accommodates a maximum of seven-digit decimal points. The *double* data type is more preferred in calculations because its wider range provides greater flexibility.

The *boolean* data type is used for making true or false declarations. These statements are common in testing environments that often require conditional verdicts. As for the *char* data type, it is designed for use in the storage of single-character data. The characters are positioned between single opening and closing quotation marks, like 'b', 'n', and so on.

Non-Primitive Data Types

The non-primitive category consists of data types that are developed by Java programmers because they do not exist in predefined formats like the primitive data types. The Array, the Interface, and the Class parameters are the data types that fall within this category. Notably, the String parameter is also a non-primitive data type, although it is accessed in a predefined format in Java. This classification is influenced by the String's status as a parameter that, just like the other data types in this category, describes objects.

Comparing Primitive and Non-Primitive Types

There are several differences between primitive and non-primitive data types. For example, primitive data types must be assigned values at all times, but non-primitive types are capable of operating without values. The call method of the non-primitive types, a functionality unavailable in the primitive types, is crucial for performing some specified operations. The letter case also helps differentiate the two, since the first letter in the non-primitive types is uppercase, while the first letter in the primitive types is lowercase. As seen earlier parts in this chapter, the data size forms part of the description of the primitive types. This is unlike the non-primitive types that do not require any data size tagging because they are similar in size.

Exercise

Rename the example under the local variables to HockeyTeamOutside and use the code to compile and display the values of the age and player variables in the exterior of their methods.

Solution:

```
public class  HockeyTeamOutside{

public void Hockey()

{

//local variable age

//local variable player

int age = 18;

}

public static void main(String args[])

{

System.out.println("Hockey player age is: " + age);

//local variable printing outside its method

}

}
```

Outcome:

C:\Users\RICHARD   E.   S.   TAKIM\Documents\Java   Programs>javac HockeyTeamOutside.java

HockeyTeamOutside.java:10: error: cannot find symbol

System.out.println("Hockey player age is: " + age);

                                  ^

  symbol: variable age

location: class HockeyTeamOutside

1 error

C:\Users\RICHARD E. S. TAKIM\Documents\Java Programs>

This particular compilation generated an error message because local variables cannot interact with outside methods.

Chapter Summary

- The operations of a Java program are anchored on variables, data types, and operators.

- A variable declaration specifies the data type and assigns a unique identity to its operational parameters.

- The declaration, assignment, and initialization procedures of a variable determine the type of the variable.

In the next chapter you will learn about the operations of constructors relative to methods.

Chapter Five:
Constructors

The creation of a new object in Java is often followed by its initialization. This initialization takes place through the constructor — that is, a block of Java code that helps to define the parameters of the objects created in the development environment. Although a constructor bears significant resemblance to the instance method, it should never be mistaken for a method because it does not provide a path for return type. A constructor has a similar identity to the class that houses it. This shows that the similarity of a constructor to a method lies in the syntax, while its similarity to the class lies in the naming.

The operations of a constructor occur in a sequence that initializes an object once a keyword that creates the object is invoked. This involves using the constructor to convey the introductory values for the class definitions of the instance variable. This procedure initiates the creation of a complete object. The public status of the keyword in a basic constructor code demonstrates unrestricted access to a constructor by other classes. Moreover, return type is a compulsory parameter in a constructor — void is not acceptable. The three main types of constructors are: default, no-argument, and parameterized.

Types

The structure of a Java class contains constructors by default. The default constructor automatically assigns zero configurations to the member variables within the class. Therefore, a default constructor does not have to be defined to trigger its operations. The failure to declare the definitions for the constructor prompts the Java class to deploy its automated mechanism for creating a default constructor, although it will lack specific coding parameters and field initialization capabilities. But the default constructor retreats into passive mode the moment its own constructors are defined. Scrutinize the structure of the code below to get a deeper understanding of how a default constructor works.

```
public class DefaultValue {

public DefaultValue(){

System.out.println("Default Constructor assigns a zero value to member
```

variables within a

class");

}

public static void main(String args[]) {

DefaultValue dv = new DefaultValue ();

}

}

The output for this particular code is: Default Constructor assigns a zero value to member variables within a class. The example clearly demonstrates that the default constructor directs the Java program to perform basic instructions.

The no argument constructor, usually expressed as no-arg, is different from the default constructor despite their similarities of signature. The no-arg constructor actually accommodates coding instructions, unlike the default constructor. However, it is common to come across sources that claim these two constructors are similar. This confusion can be avoided by determining whether a constructor contains a code or not.

Just as the name suggests, the parameterized constructor consists of a variety of parameters. It is considered a constructor with arguments because of the presence of these parameters. This particular constructor provides the flexibility of deployment of the developer's own values when launching fields. The example below demonstrates the coding of a default constructor.

public class ParameterizedValue {

public ParameterizedValue(String str){

//conceal String name;

System.out.println("parameterized constructor demo");

System.out.println("the root parameter is: "+str);

}

public static void main(String args[]) {

ParameterizedValue pv = new ParameterizedValue ("Novice Developer");

}

}

The output for this example is as follows: parameterized constructor demo, in line one; the root parameter, Novice Developer, in line two. This code demonstrates that parameterized constructors are crucial conveyors of object creation parameters. However, definitions that are restricted to parameterized constructors cannot be responsive to the creation of default constructors. If you look at the default constructor in the previous example, you will realize that its coding is slightly different from that of a parameterized constructor.

Overloading

The scalable capabilities of constructors provide room for overloading because of the functionality for detecting and filtering the different characteristics of parameters. For example, a constructor can detect the number or types of parameters that are operating within a class. It can even implement a specified order for implementing certain parameters. This makes it possible to incorporate multiple constructors in a particular class regardless of the signature variations of the constructors. Overloading allows developers to multitask and diversify the styles for creating objects because every single parameter is loaded with different functionalities for different implementations. Have a look at the example below to understand the coding of procedure for constructor overloading.

```
public class OverloadingConstructor{

public OverloadingConstructor(){

System.out.println("Utilize default constructor");

}

public OverloadingConstructor(int e){

System.out.println("Utilize parameter with one constructor with int value");

}

public OverloadingConstructor(String str){

System.out.println("Utilize parameter with one constructor and String object");

}
```

```
public OverloadingConstructor(int e, int u){

System.out.println("Utilize parameter with two constructors");

}

public static void main(String a[]){

OverloadingConstructor udc = new OverloadingConstructor();

OverloadingConstructor upc = new OverloadingConstructor(4);

OverloadingConstructor upcs = new OverloadingConstructor(4,5);

OverloadingConstructor uptc = new OverloadingConstructor("budding
developer");

}

}
```

The expected output for this particular code is Utilize default constructor, Utilize parameter with one constructor with int value, Utilize parameter with one constructor and String object, and Utilize parameter with two constructors. It is evident from the example that constructor overloading is a sort of cloning of method overloading.

Linking

The design of a constructor supports the establishment of a network of links or chains among constructors within a class. Such inter-constructor calls take place through the chaining process — that is, the utilization of a single initialization procedure to spread the influence of a parameter across various constructors. This procedure affords the developer the flexibility for restricting initialization to particular locations while exposing the user to varieties of constructors. In fact, the absence of the linking or chaining functionality would force a Java programmer to perform multiple initializations on a particular parameter to be able to trigger calls to different constructors. The example below demonstrates the coding of constructor chaining.

```
public class LinkingConstructor {

public LinkingConstructor(){
```

```
System.out.println("To the default constructor within the class");

}

public LinkingConstructor(int e){

this();

System.out.println("To a constructor with unitary parameter within the class");

}

public LinkingConstructor(int e,int u){

this(u);

System.out.println("To a constructor with two parameters within the class");

}

public static void main(String a[]){

LinkingConstructor li = new LinkingConstructor(4,5);

}

}
```

The expected outcome for this code is:

To the default constructor within the class

To a constructor with unitary parameter within the class

To a constructor with two parameters within the class

The key item in constructor linking or chaining is the 'this()' parameter. The keyword facilitates calls between constructors to implement chaining instructions.

Copying

Copying comes into play when a constructor creates and transfers the duplicate of the values of a particular object in a different object. It helps simplify programming tasks when deploying constructors with similar operational characteristics. However, the copying feature does not come installed in the constructor. It has to be written by the developer.

Constructors versus Methods

Constructors are commonly mistaken for methods due to the close relationship of the nature of their operations in an object. In fact, a constructor could easily be mistaken for a subset of a method. However, as mentioned previously, the absence of a return path in a constructor is one of the main differences between it and a method. Whereas codes have code execution capabilities for performing tasks, the role of constructors is restricted to the initialization of objects. Invocation processes in constructors take place tacitly. This is unlike methods where invocation is direct and explicit. Moreover, the flexibility to name a constructor using a similar naming convention to that of a class cannot be applied to the naming of a method. The Java compiler is capable of providing an alternative default constructor in the event of its absence. The same cannot be said of a method.

Exercise

Use a text editor to compile a no-arg constructor code and proceed to run it in the command prompt or any other relevant IDE.

Solution:

```
class NullArgument{

String s;

// parameter-free constructor

private NullArgument(){

 s = ("boat");

 System.out.println("the successful phase of building the object and s = " + ("boat"));

}

public static void main(String[] args) {

 NullArgument obj = new NullArgument();

}

}
```

This no-arg constructor code generates the following outcome: the successful phase of building the object and s = boat.

Chapter Summary

- The constructor is responsible for initializing newly created objects.

- A constructor is different from a method because it does not provide a path for return type.

- The default constructor bears built-in automated mechanisms for launching operations.

In the next chapter you will learn how to implement Object-Oriented Programming in Java.

Chapter Six:
Object-Oriented Programming in Java

Object-Oriented Programming (OOPs) is the guiding concept of the Java language. Knowledge of OOPs and its core principles is useful in the process of learning and understanding Java. OOPs entails organizing programs on the basis of data parameters, such that instructions provide the definition of data and specifies the manipulations to be performed on the data. This chapter provides a detailed discussion of the four core characteristics of OOPs including encapsulation, polymorphism, inheritance, and data abstraction.

Encapsulation

Encapsulation in Java programming involves the establishment of links between codes and data. The encapsulation process creates a chain between codes and the data that has been designated for manipulation. The OOPs environment provides the infrastructure for linking codes and data into unitary units. This process culminates in the creation of a black box containing wrapped codes and data. The transformation of code and data into a linked format actually forms an object which acts as a supporting platform for encapsulation. The object is tuned to operate on the default code or alternatively change the settings for accessing data to either a private or public state. A private default setting restricts code or data accessibility to another program within the object. A public default setting, on the other hand, allows access by programs that are external to the object. The public access programs act as channels for interacting with the private programs in the object.

Class is the primary unit of encapsulation in Java programming. A class provides object format descriptions for purposes of generating specifications for data and the corresponding codes for manipulating the data. In simpler terms, the construction of objects in Java depends on the class-generated instructions and specifications. The class contains its own codes and data that are known as members, while the data definitions that are generated by a class are commonly referred to as member variables. These member variables are in turn acted upon by codes that are known as methods.

There are various advantages associated with the encapsulation trait of OOPs.

For example, encapsulation allows users to deploy the read- or write-only conversion when in need of sidestepping the limitations to the getter or setter methods. It also contains mechanisms for exposing data to the direct control of Java programmers. For example, the dynamics of the setter method are such that a developer can set preferences on the value parameters of data by simply writing the logic instructions in the method. Encapsulation also helps conceal data from other classes that are not meant to interact with other classes in a particular object. The availability of a path for testing functionalities, alongside the automated getter- or setter-generation capabilities in IDEs, sumx up the user-friendly attributes of encapsulation.

```java
public class Encapsulate{
//private variable declaration
//access restricted to
//public class methods
private String carName;
private int carVin;
//get method for vin to facilitate accessibility
//private variable carVin
public int getVin()
{
return carVin;
}
//get method for name to facilitate accessibility
//private variable carName
public String getName()
{
return carName;
}
```

```
//set method for name to facilitate accessibility

//private variable carVin

public void setVin(int newVin)

{

carVin = newVin;

}


//set method for name to facilitate accessibility

//private variable carName

public void setName(String newName)

{

carName = newName;

}

}
```

The example above compiles in Javac but generates an error if you run it in Java. The reason behind this discrepancy is because the code does not contain the main method declaration to generate a coding outcome for the Java program. The encapsulation process requires the compilation of additional parameters that will provide the getter and setter methods for accessing individual classes in the program. The setter and getter methods for this particular example would appear like the one below.

```
public class TestingEncapsulate{

public static void main(String args[]){

Encapsulate itm = new Encapsulate();

itm.setName("Ford");

itm.setVin(123123);

System.out.println(" car Name: " + itm.getName());

System.out.println("car Vin: " + itm.getVin());
```

}

}

Note that this particular segment has a main method declaration and its class name has been changed to TestingEncapsulate. However, this segment cannot compile or run on its own. It must be joined to the first segment so that it can complete the circuit of the setter and getter methods for accessing the private data. As such, we will copy/paste the second segment on top of the javac-compiled Encapsulate.java file to introduce the main class declaration. Copy/pasting it at the bottom would generate an error message and fail to compile. It is equally important to note that although we will have TestingEncapsulate at the top alongside the main method declaration, the javac-compiled file will retain the Encapsulate.java name.

```java
public class TestingEncapsulate{

public static void main(String args[]){

Encapsulate itm = new Encapsulate();

itm.setName("Ford");

itm.setVin(123123);

System.out.println(" car Name: " + itm.getName());

System.out.println("car Vin: " + itm.getVin());

}

}

public class Encapsulate{

//private variable declaration

//access restricted to

//public class methods

private String carName;

private int carVin;

//get method for vin to facilitate accessibility
```

```java
//private variable carVin
public int getVin()
{
return carVin;
}


//get method for name to facilitate accessibility
//private variable carName
public String getName()
{
return carName;
}


//set method for name to facilitate accessibility
//private variable carVin
public void setVin(int newVin)
{
carVin = newVin;
}
//set method for name to facilitate accessibility
//private variable carName
public void setName(String newName)
{
carName = newName;
}
}
```

The output for the code will be as follows.

car Name: Ford

car Vin: 123123

Objects and Classes

The use of objects and classes to implement encapsulation is meant to create secure and controlled operations in single units of programming. Since Java is essentially an object-driven programming language and platform, these objects are real life items like cars or books that can be quantified using values, digits, or counts. The only exceptions for deviating from the quantitative reference to objects in Java occur when using the primitive-type parameters to describe data. Since objects are derived from classes, particular types of objects bear similar properties to the particular class from which they were generated.

The class carries the properties or declarations that describe the characteristics of particular types of objects. There are different types of classes and some of them can be used in the development of real-time software solutions. These classes could be anonymous, nested, or any other types that are designed for use in Java programming. A class has within it several elements including modifiers, class name, and body, among others. The modifier describes whether a class is accessible publicly or not. If the access is not public, it provides default private access declaration. The Class name component requires that initial letters be capitalized when labeling classes. The body component specifies that a class name must be positioned inside opening and closing braces like {}.

Constructors, fields, and methods are the other aspects of objects and classes that a Java beginner must understand to be able to hasten the process of learning the programming language. Whereas constructs provide the mechanisms that facilitate the initialization of objects, fields are responsible for identifying the different classes and their respective objects. Methods are the techniques that are applied to the process of controlling the behaviors or operations of classes and their objects. These methods are discussed in greater detail in the fifth chapter of this book.

Inheritance in Java

In Java programming, main classes are capable of transferring their traits to subsidiary ones through a process known as inheritance. The subsidiary, or baby, classes usually bear similar traits to those of the parent classes. Such processes that recreate classes are crucial in application development because they facilitate the creation of new class categories. The process of replicating class traits also provides the convenience of manipulating, expanding, and redeploying the methods and fields that reside in the preferred classes.

The newly created classes are not one-hundred percent similar to the parent class. Each class has its own unique attributes and the inheritance process only serves to transfer the shared traits. This simplifies coding for developers because they avoid the duplication of shared class traits and concentrate on the development of unique traits when creating subclasses. The syntax structure best demonstrates the nature of the transfer of the data profile of the members and methods of a class from the main class to the subclass. The word 'extends' is inserted in the code to show that a subclass is more or less a continuation of the main class. For example, if Bee is the subclass being created from Hive, then it would simply be expressed as 'Bee extends Hive'.

```
class Transport{

void commute() {System.out.println("commuting");}

}

class Train extends Transport{

void city() {System.out.println("intercity");}

}

class InheritanceSampling{

public static void main(String args[]){

Train t=new Train();

t.city();

t.commute();

}
```

}

Run the program above in Javac to compile and create its class. If you run the program in Java, it will generate a "can't find main(String[]) method in class" error. To run the code successfully in Java, — that is, java filename.java — transfer the block of the code containing the main(String[]) method to the top section.

```
public static void main(String args[]){

Train t=new Train();

t.city();

t.commute();

}

}


class Transport{

void commute() {System.out.println("commuting");}

}

class Train extends Transport{

void city() {System.out.println("intercity");}

}
```

The code will deliver the outcome below.

intercity

commuting

The inheritance of traits between the main and subclass is subject to limitations when the members or methods in question are declared as private. The direct transfer of traits is restricted to the public members or methods within a class. Indirect paths have to be used to open up the private attributes of the parent class to the subsidiary class. In fact, access to the private traits of the main class by the subclass is only possible through the use of protected methods residing in the former. But this type of inheritance does not expose the private data members or methods beyond the subclass. The acquired protected traits become accessible to only the sub and the parent class.

Main class to subclass transfer of traits may occur in single inheritance and multiple inheritance forms as well as multilevel, hierarchical, multiple, and hybrid inheritance formats. The single format of inheritance is a direct relationship in which the subclass draws its operational parameters directly from the main class. It is referred to as single inheritance because the relationship of extending traits occurs between one parent class and one subclass at a time.

Multilevel inheritance prevails when the subclass exists as an extension of the main class. It occurs in a linear structure whereby the parent class shares its traits to a chain of offshoots. In other words, the main class passes its characteristics to the subclass, which in turn shares the attributes to its offshoot, and so on. Just like a family or genealogy tree, this chain can stretch and spread out to an extent where the class at the top of the chain would become the ancestor class.

```
class Transport{

void commute() {System.out.println("commuting");}

}

class Train extends Transport{

void city() {System.out.println("intercity");}

}

class Ticket extends Train{

void discount() {System.out.println("discounting");}

}

class InheritanceSampling{

public static void main(String args[]){

Ticket t=new Ticket();

t.discount();

t.city();

t.commute();
```

}

}

Run the program above in Javac to compile and create its class. If you run the program in Java, it will generate a "can't find main(String[]) method in class" error. To run the code successfully in Java, — that is, java filename.java — transfer the block of the code containing the main(String[]) method to the top section.

```
class InheritanceSampling{

public static void main(String args[]){

Ticket t=new Ticket();

t.discount();

t.city();

t.commute();

}

}

class Transport{

void commute() {System.out.println("commuting");}

}

class Train extends Transport{

void city() {System.out.println("intercity");}

}

class Ticket extends Train{

void discount() {System.out.println("discounting");}

}
```

The code will deliver the outcome below.

discounting

intercity

commuting

Hierarchical inheritance does not follow the linear pattern. Instead, this form of single inheritance shares its traits to several subclasses at the same time. It is similar to a situation of twins, triplets, or quadruplets inheriting their traits from their parent.

The multiple type inheritance, on the other hand, differs from the single inheritance format in the manner in which inheritance is channeled from the main class to the subclass. It is actually the opposite of hierarchical inheritance, such that it is the subclass that shares the traits of several main classes. That is exactly what happens when a child inherits the traits of both parents. However, Java does not provide support for this kind of inheritance.

There are occasions when a single program can accommodate two or more types of inheritance at the same time. For example, a single program could feature single hierarchical and multilevel inheritance simultaneously. This results in a hybrid type of inheritance because of the pattern of different classes and subclasses sharing extended members and methods. To get a clear picture of this pattern, imagine hierarchically-oriented subclasses XYZ extending class Q, which in turn extends multilevel-oriented subclasses R and S. Such combinations of the different types of inheritance are considered to by hybrid because the traits of the main classes are extended beyond the linear or branching barriers of the inheritance relationships.

Method overriding is also a common occurrence in inheritance operations. That is because of the possibility of making identical method declarations in both the parent class and the subsidiary class. The method overriding process essentially involves triggering a call to a method in the subsidiary class, although it is already present in the main class. This allows developers to call a specified method from within the subsidiary class rather than making reference to the parent class. However, it is still possible to initiate a method call to the parent class through the use of a super keyword.

Dimension of Constructors in Inheritance

Some of the aspects of constructors, as discussed in the previous chapter, are significantly relevant to inheritance processes in Java. The creation of the object of a subsidiary class automatically invokes the constructor of that subsidiary class, before subsequently invoking the constructor of the parent class. Since the actions are designed to run by default, object construction follows the sequential pattern whereby the constructors at the lower level of the hierarchy (subsidiary objects) inherit shared attributes from the ones at the top (parent objects).

The dynamics of constructors in inheritance operations are anchored on the super keyword. This keyword is always positioned at the head of a constructor's statement to provide the descriptive parameters to the main class. This actually prioritizes the main class over the other subclasses in the hierarchy of inheritance. The super keyword does not support interactions between a parent class and subclasses that are strange to it. Such interactions are restricted to the main class associated with the subclasses that have inherited its traits. It is also possible to prevent the inheritance of the data members or methods of a parent class through the use of the final keyword. This particular keyword seals off the parent class and triggers error messages whenever a subclass attempts to execute an extension operation.

The inheritance principle as a whole has so far demonstrated that close relationships exist between the parent classes and subsidiary classes in Java programming. This relationship cascades down to the relationship among objects in a program, and that is the reason behind the relevance of the constructors in establishing hierarchy between the parent and subsidiary classes when deploying data members and methods in objects.

Polymorphism in Java

Polymorphism is a principle of OOPs that refers to the transformational flexibility of objects. It describes the ability of objects to change into a variety of forms according to the demands of the programming environment. For example, if a professional expert were to be perceived through the polymorphism lenses, then we would be looking at the person's ability to adjust comfortably to different responsibilities such as accounting, systems administration, and procurement in the finance and administration department. Therefore, polymorphism is simply the ability to wear many hats, metaphorically speaking. In Java programming, polymorphism removes limits on the scope of actions or instructions. There are always options and alternatives to performing particular actions or carrying out specific instructions.

Polymorphism allows Java programmers to source multiple implementations for a single definition because the display or conveyance of messaging can assume different formats. As such, once the message is channeled to the designated interface, it can follow one of the many paths required to create the reference variables for translating the message to the desired context. Polymorphism, just like inheritance, provides for the extension of attributes between the main class and the subclass.

Java programmers mainly interact with polymorphism during compile time or runtime operations when building applications. The polymorphism that occurs during compile time is known as static binding, while the one that occurs during runtime is known as dynamic binding. Static binding and dynamic binding are associated with method overloading and method overriding, respectively. Factors such as control over the flow of definitions and the filtering of parameters are crucial in determining the nature of polymorphism operations. Whereas compile time operations generally provide the flexibility for handling multiple definitions and parameters, runtime operations are more suited for injecting the inheritance perspective in the implementation of methods. Therefore, method overloading and overriding in Java play distinctive roles despite both belonging to the broader boundaries of polymorphism.

Method Overloading

The operation decisions in method overloading are decided during compilation time whenever static binding is in action. Polymorphism is accommodative to method overloading because of multiplicity of definitions relative to the interfaces for message channeling and implementations. Overloading prevails when a method accepts multiple variables with shared identities but varying parameters. A method that houses multiple identical definitions is equally capable of executing the underlying varying parameters of the definitions.

The sources of multiple definitions with identical names would usually be instructions that are conveyed to the method. For example, an instruction to create a contact in a mobile phone would normally aim at saving a single mobile phone number in the phonebook. However, the instruction could instead convey two mobile phone numbers simultaneously, prompting the method to save the two contacts. But rather than save the two contacts separately, the method will accommodate both contacts under a single identity. Let's explore another example using computation operators for calculations shown below.

```
public class Census{

int multiply(int a, int b){

return a*b;

}

int multiply(int d, int e, int f){

return d*e*f;

}

}


class Population{

public static void main(String args[]){

Census pop = new Census();

System.out.println(pop.multiply(2, 3));

System.out.println(pop.multiply(4, 5, 3));

}

}
```

This javac-compiled code contains two separate methods with varied lists sharing the 'multiply' name. The compile time operations dictate the selection and order of the implementation of the methods. Attempt running the code in a java filename.java format to generate the results of the computation and compare your answer with the exercise at the end of this chapter.

As such, a method overloads to execute additional parameters instead of triggering an error message. The variations of parameters manifest in type and count. Differences that are based on the types of method parameters concern the nature of parameters that are selected for execution. And because overloading is a compile time decision, the object gets to select the target method for execution upon the determination and conveyance of parameters to the program. As for the differences that are based on the count of method parameters, the functionality of the method provides flexibility for processing multiple parameters. But the selection of the particular method to be executed will be determined by the parameters conveyed to the program, this being a compile time polymorphism operation.

Method overloading is also closely related to operator overloading — that is, the attachment of a variety of meanings to similar operators or symbols. Although Java does not support operator overloading, there are alternative mechanisms that are used to achieve indirect implementation of this type of overloading. For example, the plus (+) operator can be applied to two different sets of strings to achieve multiple conveyances of definitions. This particular operator can be applied in the summation of integers or linkage of subsidiary sets of strings as well. Such a mechanism basically creates a chain between two strings that are subsidiary to a main string. This shows that unlike method overloading, which provides direct paths for establishing relationships between definitions and parameters, operator overloading in Java requires a bit of customizations.

Method Overriding

Method overriding arises when a subsidiary class creates similar implementation methods to that of a parent class. This results in a situation where the implementation methods of the subclass exist on top of those of the main class. The implementation method of the subsidiary class actually extends the implementation method of the parent class. This allows developers to manipulate the composition of methods in the subclass by creating inheritance channels with the main class. Method overriding is the driving force behind dynamic polymorphism because it supports the execution of overridden methods during runtime operations, as demonstrated in this javac-compiled example.

```
public class ComputerTraining{

public void courses () {

System.out.println("Basic Packages");

}

}
```

```java
class Photoshop extends ComputerTraining {

public void courses() {

System.out.println("Basic Packages");

}

}

class CorelDraw extends ComputerTraining{

//method overriding in action

public void courses(){

System.out.println("New segment of Packages");

}

}
```

The courses() method has provided a single path for providing definitions to the subsidiary classes that would otherwise have required the creation of a new method for every new segment of packages. Photoshop contains the basic package definition. CorelDraw has both the basic and the new package definitions, and that is what method overriding is all about. To better understand the process, let's introduce a main class method to the javac-compiled example above to be able to run it as Java and observe the outcome.

```java
class OverridingDemo{

public static void main(String args[]){

Coreldraw c=new Coreldraw();

c.courses();

}

}


public class ComputerTraining{

public void courses () {

System.out.println("Basic Packages");
```

```
}

}

class Photoshop extends ComputerTraining {

public void courses() {

System.out.println("Basic Packages");

}

}

class Coreldraw extends ComputerTraining{

//method overriding in action

public void courses(){

System.out.println("New Segment of Packages");

}

}
```

The outcome of this code will be:

New Segment of Packages

Therefore, overriding is a runtime decision because the object gets to select the target method for execution upon the invocation of the overriding method. It is basically a choice between executing a method residing in the main class or calling a method residing in the subclass. This is dictated by the type of object and its designated instructions for calling either the subclass or the main class. The developer sets the pace of these runtime operations by specifying the operational definitions of the subclass relative to the main class. For example, the developer must state the relationship between the object of the subsidiary class and reference of the parent class to facilitate the selection of the appropriate method that the object would call during the runtime operations. And the object will call the method in the subclass because execution in this case will be subject to the method in the subclass rather than the reference parameters in the main class.

There are various benefits of deploying dynamic polymorphism, such as method overriding, in Java programming. For example, the ability of a class to profile and prescribe methods for all its subsidiary classes depends on the runtime operations of dynamic polymorphism. Moreover, dynamic polymorphism is instrumental in the acquisition of methods and definitions of method implementations in the subsidiary classes.

Abstraction in Java

Abstraction is a component of OOPs that focuses on the 'what' rather than the 'how' of data operations in Java. It involves the concealment of the intricate and complex aspects of the operations behind the performance of programs. Users only get to interact with the levels that facilitate the launch and functioning of programs. A good example of a real life situation is a PC.

The user logs into the PC, opens files, keys information, and saves the files in designated drives without having to bother with how the computer programs work to facilitate those operations. There are so many programs that work in the background but they are completely hidden from the user. That is what abstraction entails in Java programming — exposing to the user the functions of objects but hiding the details about the design and architecture of those functions.

Abstraction is not meant to disenfranchise the user. It is actually designed to enhance efficiency, simplicity, and security by exposing only the essential components of programs and concealing the unnecessary ones. This makes it possible for the Java programmer to determine the information that would be important to the user and ensure that only that information is exposed to the user. It is important for the programmer to be able to build data categories according to their significance and relevance to the user. Indeed, there are many technical details of how programs work that users may find complicated to understand or irrelevant to their tasks. It is up to the programmer to provide the necessary filtration mechanisms through abstraction.

Classes, methods, and interfaces are the core components of implementing abstraction in Java. The interface is designed to facilitate the implementation of inheritances in abstraction processes. It is particularly useful in handling multiple inheritances and is meant to accommodate strictly public abstract methods. However, its use is characterized by many limitations that include an inability to implement abstract classes and providing only public static final classes. The abstraction interface is less flexible compared to the abstract class, which supports a greater scope of support for different operations and functionalities. Except for the fact that the abstract class structure is not compliant to multiple inheritances, it supports all the other operations that the interface rejects.

Abstract Class

Although the classes and methods are discussed under the other three principles of OOPs already, they are still the core of abstraction operations. In fact, abstraction should not be confused with encapsulation because, whereas the former conceals a whole load of details, that latter only conceals data. Abstraction goes beyond just binding and concealing data categories to expose user interfaces required to exploit functionalities. Therefore, abstraction is more design-oriented while encapsulation is more implementation-oriented.

The use of an abstract keyword is all that is needed to declare an abstract class. Such a declaration means that there are no mechanisms for instantiating a particular class. The lack of instantiation procedures is the reason behind the unavailability of objects in abstract classes. An abstract class is capable of operating with or without abstract methods in it. This means that an abstract class can accommodate solid and abstract methods separately or in combination. A class is declared abstract if it contains a combination of both solid and abstract methods. But the requirements are different for a normal class because it maintains the status quo if it does not host any abstract methods.

Constructors form part of the operational profile of the abstract class. The constructors could be default or parameterized. The default constructor is a requisite component of the abstract class, while the parameterized one is optional. The other important fact about the abstract class is that it accepts both static and final methods. This provides Java programmers broader options for designing method implementations.

The use cases of the abstract class revolve around the structuring needs of the parent class relative to the derived classes. It is about the scope of the properties that can be transferred from the parent to the subsidiary class. Abstraction comes in handy because it provides the mechanism for hiding the information that should not be shared to the subclass. In most cases, the parent class normally transfers generic or skeleton kinds of structure to the subclass for the latter to generate the rest of the details.

Abstract Method

A method is declared abstract if it operates without a body — that is, the parameters for defining inputs and outputs of method operations. The abstract class serves as the destination point for all declared abstract methods. However, this declaration does not constitute the end of the operations of the abstract methods because they are not capable of executing implementations. The abstract class is also responsible for implementing the abstract methods that are contained within it.

When a method manipulates the definition of a subclass, it imposes the need for the implementation of method overriding to address the relationship between the abstract methods of the subclass and the main class. As such, the presence of an abstract method is a precursor to the compulsory implementation of inheritance between subsidiary classes and the main classes. In the event that a concrete subsidiary class is used to extend the properties of an abstract main class, the respective subsidiary class must acquire and execute the implementation of the abstract methods contained in the parent. Alternatively, the developer could transform the definitions of the subclass to abstract status to eliminate definition overlaps with the main class.

The use cases of the abstract method are centered on the profiles and declarations of subclasses. It is particularly useful in situations where multiple classes perform similar operations using different parameters. The abstract method helps in defining and breaking down these complex procedures for implementation by the abstract class. The abstract method's support for extending the properties of the abstract class is significantly useful in managing the inheritance of properties between concrete subsidiary classes and abstract main classes. These methods must be present for the concrete class to be able to spread the abstract properties to the entire set of methods that constitutes the main class.

Exercise

Refer to the method overloading segment under the Polymorphism in Java subheading of this chapter and run the javac-compiled example in that segment as a java filename.java format in your command prompt.

Solution:

```java
class Population{

public static void main(String args[]){

Census pop = new Census();

System.out.println(pop.multiply(2, 3));

System.out.println(pop.multiply(4, 5, 3));

}

}


public class Census{

int multiply(int a, int b){

return a*b;

}

int multiply(int d, int e, int f){

return d*e*f;

}

}
```

Output:

6

60

Chapter Summary

- The core OOPs principles include encapsulation, inheritance, polymorphism, and abstraction.

- Encapsulation allows the developer to establish links between codes and data.

- Polymorphism concerns the transformational characteristics of objects.

- Inheritance is the transfer of data characteristics between parent and subsidiary objects.

- Abstraction describes the scope of data operations in a Java program.

In the next chapter you will learn the procedure for implementing modules in Java.

Chapter Seven:
Modules in Java

The Java module, also known as Project Jigsaw, is a collection of packages. It is one of the highlight features that were introduced with the release of Java 9. This particular program underwent development and piloting for several years before it was finally included in the Java 9 release. The program was slated for launch with Java 7 and later with Java 8, but failed on both occasions due to unknown reasons in the public domain that led to the delays. The Java module has since become a crucial aspect of software development.

A Java module facilitates the bundling of applications and packages in a way that controls the functionality of the packages. As such, a Java module is created when the applications and packages are transformed into a single suit. The Java module moderates the visibility of its packages to other Java modules. This way, the Java module is able to determine the packages that can be accessed or reused by other modules on the one hand, and the specific modules it must interact with to complete tasks on the other. The program achieves the controlled distribution through the segmentation of packages into either exported or concealed categories. Exported packages are readily exposed to access and interaction with other packages within a module. Concealed packages are restricted to the internal coding operations of the module and cannot interact with external packages.

Advantages of Java Modules

The Java module provides significant advantages for Java programmers. For example, the feature was introduced to enhance efficiency in the reuse of classes and save Java programmers the efforts of writing new codes. The inheritance properties and interface capabilities are the crucial elements that facilitate the reuse of classes and objects.

Fragmentation of the Java modules into autonomous units makes it easier for developers to determine and select the preferred specifications for applications. This helps decongest the Java development environment because developers have the flexibility to limit selections to the modules that are required for particular applications. This is a departure from the pre-Java 9 versions that lumped many APIs and applications together because they lacked mechanisms for predicting the classes that would be required in the programming processes. The increased use of Java in small or handheld devices like mobile phones and tablets has necessitated the development of light-weight and fragmented solutions, such as the Java module, for packaging applications.

Missing Java modules trigger error warnings during startup. In fact, the JVM cannot launch operations if it detects missing modules. This allows developers to make corrections well in advance as opposed to experiencing the inconvenience of unexpected module gaps during runtime. Late discovery of a missing module may prompt a developer to abandon a work-in-progress and start an application development process all over again. This was mostly the case in pre-Java 9 series.

Objectives of Java Modules

The modularization of Java 9 was informed by various objectives that included the consolidation of configuration parameters, strengthening of encapsulation, condensation of Java's scalability and integrity, and the enhancement of performance. All these factors contributed to the elevation of the modular programs to a higher level that packages because of the greater functionalities that they introduced to Java programming.

Configuration upgrades through the modularity solution were needed to implement dependency declarations that were capable of hastening compilation and execution processes. Strengthened encapsulation simplified the management of packages and their relationship to the modules with respect to managing data accessibility within programs. There was urgent need for a solution that was capable of supporting explicit declarations of the capabilities that were required to facilitate interactions between different modules. The limitations imposed on the minimum interaction requirements are useful in enhancing the security of the Java platform.

The scaling aspect organized the previously scattered Java programs and tools into a specific number of modules that can be identified with ease. The scaled properties of the modules provide greater flexibility for customizing the scope of module utilization. The platform integrity objective eliminated the deployment of unnecessary apps during application development processes. Modularization streamlined app deployment through the introduction of encapsulation mechanisms for concealing the classes. Enhanced performance was definitely the overall objective of the modularization transformation. The Java 9 modules provide predictive tools for determining the exact modules needed for particular programming activities, and this allows the JVM to operate more efficiently.

Insights into the Structure of Java 9 Module

According to Deitel (n.d.), the Java module was initially launched as Project Jigsaw, but was later renamed and modularized into Java 9 where it sits on top of packages. This module requires developers to observe certain conditions when building applications using Java 9. For example, a unique naming system is used in addition to the provision of specific descriptions of its dependencies.

A Java module consists of a directory structure, a declarator, and a source code. The three items actually form the sequence for creating a Java module. There are specifications for creating a directory structure and declaring the module, but the specifications of the directory structure are not significantly different from the specifications that are applied in the creation of Java packages. However, it is important to remember that a module and the sources of the module bear a similar name that is modeled on a reverse domain pattern. For example, a Sample Coding preferred unique name of the module would appear as: com.samplecoding.

The declarator hosts the metadata definitions of the dependencies of a module alongside the packages that the module is capable of extending to other modules. It actually exists as the compiled format of a module declaration as per the definitions contained in the module-info.java file. The keyword 'module' appears as the compulsory first word in a declaration.

A unique name that follows the module facilitates its identification from other modules. An ideal descriptor name would appear as follows: *module modulename*, followed by an opening curly brace at the end of the name and a closing curly brace that is aligned to the left below the name. If we use the Sample Coding name as the unique identification of the module, the descriptor name would appear as follows:

module com.samplecoding{

}

The body of the declaration is positioned between the two curly braces, but the body segment is optional as you may choose to leave it empty or include commands for performing specific operations such as *exports*, *opens*, *provides*, and *requires*. The other widely used commands include: *uses*, *to*, and *with*. As such, a module name and opening and closing curly braces are sufficient to a construct a declarator. The module creation process involves several steps that require you to construct a directory structure, declarator, and a source code.

- Step one: We will follow the widely practiced format and use the src as the root directory for our source files. Create the src directory, label it with the unique name of the module, and save. In this particular example, the src is the equivalent of the uniquely named module file — that is, com.samplecoding. But you still need to create the com.samplecoding folder and save it in the src folder to comply with the recommended module structure.

- Step two: Create a module-info.java text editor file and execute an empty module declaration within that file. Remember that the name of the declared module should be similar to the name of the directory that houses it. In this example, this step simply involves making the com.samplecoding declaration inside a module-info.java program file, and saving it in the src folder.

- Step three: In the com.samplecoding, split the reverse domain from the module name and use each of the two parts to create two folders. Start with the com folder and store it in the com.samplecoding folder. Proceed to create a samplecoding folder and store it in the com folder. At this point the module structure has transformed as follows: the src folder contains the com.samplecoding folder, which in turn houses the com folder and the module-info.java file. The com folder contains the samplecoding folder, which in turn will store a source code of the Java program to be compiled in the next step.

- Step four: Open a new text editor and construct a source code of your choice. This example is using SampleItem and SampleItem.java as the class and file name, respectively. Save the program file in the samplecoding folder with the SampleItem.java name, while the rest of the files will maintain their names and positions in the directory structure.

public class SampleItem{

public static void main(String[] args){

System.out.println("Sample item for testing Java module");

}

}

- Step five: Compile the module in javac to create a class file. The compilation process involves the use of a command. For this particular example, the command would read as follows: javac –d mods --module-source-path src/ --module com.samplecoding. This converts the module-info.java and SampleItem.java files into module-info.class and SampleItem.class, respectively. The compilation procedure will also replace the src with mods as the root directory.

Exercise

Steps one to three provide a detailed description of a module structure. Use the description to create a diagram of the module structure.

Solution:

src

com.samplecoding

module-info.java   com

samplecoding

SampleItem.java

Chapter Summary

- The Java module was initially unveiled as Project Jigsaw and was introduced alongside Java 9.

- The Java module contains a variety of packages that allow developers to determine and control the functionality of Java programs.

- A Java module is labeled using a unique naming system and specific descriptions of its dependencies.

In the next chapter you will learn the underlying concepts of asynchronous programming.

Chapter Eight:
Parallel Programming in Java

Synchronous programming occurs when the CPU performs one method at a time in an orderly sequence, such that one task has to be completed before the next one launches. The completion of the current task automatically triggers the commencement of the next task. In parallel programming, also known as asynchronous programming, the situation is the opposite of what happens in the synchronous programming patterns. The execution of methods does not follow a sequence in asynchronous programming; several methods can be executed simultaneously during the performance of tasks. As such, it is possible for the program to run other applications alongside the basic application thread. Other than tasks and threads, pipelines and non-blocking calls are the other crucial elements of asynchronous programming.

The thread is the primary building block for implementing asynchronous programming concepts. A Java programmer can use single thread or multi-threaded codes when writing programs. The functionality of a thread within a CPU concerns the capacity of a processor to accommodate multiple sets of synchronous activities simultaneously or in parallel. There are restrictions on the number of tasks that can run parallel within a CPU because of the limitation on the availability of threads. The situation is a bit different if the threads are domiciled in the operating system because it is scalable and capable of accommodating the hefty traffic of threads that are running parallel.

CompletionStage API

The CompletionStage API for asynchronous programming in Java resides in the JDK. CompletionStage refers to the phase in asynchronous programming, whereby the completion of a parallel computation paves the way for the launch of other related phases. This is because the communication that occurs during task performances allows the secondary threads to report the progress and completion of tasks to the primary thread.

CompletableFuture

Prior to Java 8 release, portals such as Future and Callback interfaces were widely used to implement asynchronous programs. Although these interfaces were meant to simplify the complex computations of the asynchronous programs, they did not achieve the desired results. For example, when the Future interface was added in Java 5, it lacked combination mechanisms for computations and effective error-handling capabilities.

The introduction of the CompletableFuture was a game changer that was unveiled in the Java 8 release. It essentially provides an operational phase for exposing steps in asynchronous programming that can be deployed in combination with other computation procedures to deliver solutions. The use of the CompletableFuture in combination of the Future interface addresses the shortfalls of the earlier Java versions. The CompletableFuture features bulky class parameters consisting of powerful frameworks hosting tens of methods that are designed to simplify asynchronous computations. This enhances its flexibility for deploying methods for different operations including task combinations and error handling. However, the bulky nature of the CompletableFuture should not be a source of concern for a Java programmer because its architecture is tailored to respond on a case-by-case basis to avoid the burden of running operations that are not required or resourceful.

The public interface of the CompletableFuture class organizes its operations in sequences that ensure a new phase begins only after the completion of a previous one. A phase is considered complete upon the termination of its computation. This means that the completion of a current computation or instruction is what triggers the commencement of the next one, and the delay in a predecessor task delays the commencement of the successor task as well. The public interface consists of a few fundamental pillars that branch out into a wider scope of methods that are suited for various styles or uses.

Whenever a given phase of the public interface performs a prescribed function, it uses expressions such as 'function' to describe things like requisite constructors and outcomes. However, the execution aspect is a bit different with respect to the sequence of occurrence, because there are occasions when two phases can be executed simultaneously. This happens when the outcome of the successor stage is crucial in validating the outcome of the predecessor phase. As such, whereas the completion of the computation of the predecessor stage could as well signal the commencement of the successor stage, the execution of the predecessor stage remains pending until the successor stage executes to provide data validation.

The issue of dependency between different phases and its impact on the order of computation does not dictate the order in which the execution events may occur. The phase-by-phase trigger of events is actually limited to computation because order of execution varies with the nature and scope of each of the phases. An Oracle (2019) documentation description titled "All Known Implementing Classes: CompletableFuture" mentioned default, default asynchronous, and custom executions as the main arrangement formats that executions may take. The order of occurrence of events in the default execution and default asynchronous execution is determine by the parameters of implementing the CompletionStage API rather than CompleteFuture's public interface. The custom execution relies more on the dynamics of a supplied Executor (Oracle, 2019) that contains parameters for accommodating asynchronous implementations.

Chapter Summary

- Asynchronous programming supports the simultaneous execution of multiple methods during the task performance.

- Asynchronous programming uses the thread as the primary building block of implementing its concepts.

- The completionStage API is responsible for moderating operations in asynchronous programming.

In the next chapter you will learn about parsing and its significance in Java programming.

Chapter Nine:
Java Parsers

There are occasions when chunks of data have to be split into smaller sizes to simplify manipulation or facilitate interpretation. In Java programming, such data is split through a process known as parsing. The parsing procedure is implemented on the basis instructions that define the scope and limits for breaking down the data. Parsing is done with the help of a parser — that is, a program that is specifically designed for use in data breakdown processes.

Parsing is not restricted to Java programming; it is similarly deployable in other programming languages. Moreover, the suitability of a particular parser to break down a particular block of data depends on the nature of the data in question. A Java program has the discretion to determine the parser that would be best suited to break data. There are various alternatives of parsers including a predesigned library-based parser, manually customized parsers, or a library-based parser created by the developer.

A predesigned library-based parser is basically an existing parser that is meant to support a specific language — in this case, the Java language. In Java, this particular parser features a variety of tools, such as APIs, that make it easier for developers to implement modifications or enhancements using the programming language. The manually customized parser is meant for use in dismantling data blocks that cannot be handled by the conventionally generated parsers. It is about a programmer developing a parser and tailoring its functionalities to suit unique needs. As for the library-based parser created by the developer, it provides greater flexibility to generate a parser compared to the deployment of rigid existing libraries.

Parsers are also identified according to the structure of their body or coding. For example, a parser that processes data in textual format is a text parser while one that executes data in XML or JavaScript Object Notation (JSON) format is XML parser. The text parser is appropriate for procedures involving the transformation and consumption of text-formatted data inputs. The XML parser, on the other hand, is useful in interpreting the XML or JSON data parameters. As such, the XML parser involves more complex data processing operations compared to the text parser.

Simple API for XML

Developers using parsers have a variety of choices at their disposal. There is the sequential parser that restricts operations to current events, and a developer can neither navigate backwards to access data that has been parsed already nor skip to the next data parsing event before completing the current one. The Simple API for XML, or SAX, is one such sequence-controlled parser that developers can interact with when building Java applications. There are many more examples depending on the nature of the applications undergoing development. To get a better understanding of the SAX structure, familiarize yourself with the basic format of an XML document.

```
<?xml version="7.0"?>
<SAMPLIST>
<SAMP>
<SIDENTIFICATION>CAT</SIDENTIFICATION>
</SAMP>
<SAMP>
<SIDENTIFICATION>DOG</SIDENTIFICATION>
</SAMP>
</SAMPLIST>
```

SAX executes XML data on an event-by-event basis in a linear format. This means that the completion of the current event creates room for the commencement of the next one. It assumes the linear format, rather than branching out like the tree format, by conveying notifications of events during the operations for parsing elements. A SAX operation would transform the XML document on the basis of linear conventions as demonstrated in the Oracle (2019) sourced example below.

```
start document

start document: SAMPLIST
star element: SAMP
start element SIDENTIFICATION
characters: CAT
end element: SIDENTIFICATION
end element: SAMP

start document: SAMPLIST
star element: SAMP
start element SIDENTIFICATION
characters: DOG
end element: SIDENTIFICATION
end element: SAMP

end element: SAMPLIST

end document
```

The implementation of SAX in parsing requires a *SAXParser* Object, according

86

to an article published in the Oracle website as of December 2019. SAX is actually appropriately equipped with interfaces that generate call-back methods that facilitate the interpretation of event notifications during the data parsing operations. The SAX parser is suited for use in XML documents that are either bulky or require further manipulation. Its lightweight credentials provide the convenience for surface-level or readily exposable XML parsing operation. Moreover, a linear parsing format is known to work faster and more efficiently than the tree structure.

Document Object Model

The random parser provides more flexibility for navigating forward and backward when parsing data. The random parser is actually the direct opposite of the sequential parser. The Document Object Model, or XML DOM, parser falls under the random category. The DOM parser hosts the interface definitions for manipulating documents that are formatted in XML. A mere implementation of any particular interface is sufficient to trigger the writing process of the XML files. Unlike SAX's linear-formatted data, the XML DOM assumes a branching structure because of its access to a variety of methods and interfaces. As such, the tree structure offers a wide range of options for viable data parsing implementations. The diagram below shows how a basic DOM structure would look if we use the details in the XML document provided under SAX.

<SAMPLIST>	
<SAMP>	<SAMP>
<SIDENTIFICATION>	<SIDENTIFICATION>
CAT	DOG

Motivations behind the preferences for DOM include its suitability for parsing elements that are below the 1,000 count in addition to its data manipulation flexibility. It is particularly suitable for operations involving repetitive changes of elements. However, developers have to contend with its lack of support for fragmented data edits. The formation of DOM's tree structure precedes parsing operations, effectively making it difficult to implement selective manipulation once the structure takes shape. This limitation is the major reason developers may choose to avoid the DOM parser, because the tree structure tends to scuttle performance.

Chapter Summary

- Parsing is the process of splitting programs into smaller and more manageable chunks.

- A parser can be accessed in a predesigned format or customized format.

- Body structures and coding formats are crucial for identifying the type of parser in use.

In the next chapter you will learn how to apply graphical user interface toolkits in applications.

Chapter Ten:
A Guide to Java GUI Toolkits

Graphical User Interface (GUI) applications in Java are useful in the implementation of interactive and user-friendly display features in programs. The integration of graphics requires accompanying tools for facilitating the utilization of a variety of visual and display functionalities. This could be labels, buttons, or any other features that bring graphics to life in applications. There are various operational elements that provide display mechanisms during application building processes. For example, the developer's navigation through the different interfaces of an application is facilitated by tools like menus, grids, and sidebars. Input controls comprising features such as text fields and buttons are equally important. The GUI elements also facilitate access to several information parameters including icons and labels. Swing and JavaFX are the major frameworks for implementing GUI in Java applications.

Java Swing

Swing is a GUI-compliant API that was introduced to replace Java's Abstract Widget Toolkit (AWT) API. It has been an almost permanent feature in the Java SE since it was unveiled with the release of Java 1.2. The AWT was actually heavy and platform-dependent because of its design and compatibility limitations. Compared to its predecessor, Swing was packaged as a lightweight solution that provided more interactive user interfaces for multiplatform implementations. Other comparisons between Swing and the AWT show that:

- Unlike the AWT, Swing's interface is compliant to layout and appearance adjustments.

- Swing provides a broader scope of applicability because it is equipped with a wide variety of components. Lack of sufficient components was one of AWT's major undoings.

- Whereas Swing can be slowed down by the deployment of multiple components simultaneously, the AWT maintained stable speeds regardless of the increase in the number of active components.

Swing operates as a collection of elements for user interface implementation and bears a modular structure that simplifies utilization and customization of the components. Lightweight architecture has been particularly cited as Swing's highlight feature because of the convenience its toolkit provides in accessing different functionality elements of the OS. This includes interactive user capabilities found on the display devices. The lightweight structure also reflects on the ease of interacting with devices when using the mouse or keyboard shortcuts. There is also the plugging component that is equipped with extendable features for manipulating the appearance of applications. This gives the developer greater control over the determination of the general layout of the graphical components of applications. The *java.swing* package is particularly instrumental in importing the components of Swing that are responsible for facilitating seamless plug-ins into functionality features of the user interface.

Developers find Swing to be user-friendly with regards to configuration and deployment procedures. Its setup mechanisms are easy to control and accommodative to runtime manipulation of settings. The coding mostly remains untouched during the manipulation of Swing operations because it is capable of delivering desired changes with minimal alterations. Moreover, it is possible to restrict changes to a target component without affecting the composition of other components. This saves time because the developer does not have to worry about the statuses of other components when implementing changes to a target component.

Anchorage of Swing on the Model-View-Controller (MVC) platform allows it to deploy abstraction mechanisms between coding and implementation of the GUI. Developers of GUI applications generally find abstraction useful in establishing the necessary barriers between the operational functions that must remain concealed and the display functions that should be exposed to the users.

The hierarchy structure of the Swing toolkit is such that all elements fall under the JComponent which in turn is attached to a container. Such a structure simplifies the addition of elements to container classes. That is because a container class is capable of accommodating several elements within them. There are only two levels of hierarchy above the container — the component and the object which sits at the top. The application building environment of a GUI must have one or more container objects. This could be the panel, the frame, or the dialog container object. The panel container object serves the purpose of arranging components on a window. It is considered to be a pure container object because it cannot transform into a window. The frame container objects operates as a fully fledged window that comes complete with headings and icons. As for the dialog container object, it deploys pop-up mechanisms to convey message notifications. Therefore it does not possess complete window properties similar to those of the frame. The simple code below demonstrates the basic structure of the Swing toolkit.

```
import javax.swing.*;

class TestSwing{

public static void main(String[] args){

JFrame j=new JFrame("Swing Song");

j.setVisible(true);

}

}
```

Open your command prompt window and compile the program using javac to generate its class file. Proceed to run the program using Java — that is java FileName.java. This particular code will generate a pop-up window like the one below. Take note that the pop-up window is always tiny and could pass unnoticed. It is most likely to pop up at the top-left side of your screen, from where you can drag and resize it accordingly.

However, Swing has a number of flaws despite the glittering attributes compared to its predecessor and successor. Other than concerns over its tendency to slow down when exposed to multiple components, Swing is extremely delicate and requires a lot of caution from developers when using it to build GUI applications. In some occasions, it misrepresents the appearance of components, making it unreliable for organizing the layout of applications. This undermines the sophisticated look and feel credentials that are associated with Swing.

JavaFx

The first release of the JavaFX hit the scene in 2008. However, JavaFX largely remained in the shadows of Swing until the 2014 release of Java 8, which had it as the primary GUI toolkit. Although JavaFX did not entirely replace Swing, the decision to elevate it over Swing in Java 8 and the later editions was an indication of Oracle's plans to eventually retire Swing over the long term. Oracle's intentions were motivated by the greater scope of operational capabilities in JavaFX compared to Swing. The JavaFX toolkit was particularly equipped with advanced components for implementing a wide range of web programming concepts.

JavaFX allows programmers to build feature-rich applications for use in desktop and internet environments. The JavaFX toolkit can be deployed in the development of a wide range of applications including graphics, charts, and animation. It also provides a development environment for multimedia applications like video and audio. JavaFX makes it easier for developers to tailor the performance features of various applications destined for use in multimedia platforms.

The core structure of JavaFX consists of high-level frameworks and APIs that support interactions with advanced media functions and user interface features, such as the GUI, when building applications. JavaFX is synonymous with the rich client technology and hardware platforms that accelerate the processing and performance of graphics. The platform's GUI capability is characterized by modernized appearance and enhanced performance, making it a viable alternative for deployment as a client or library in Java SE and other Java platforms.

The JavaFX APIs are extremely crucial to the process of designing, creating, and testing GUI applications. These APIs could be helpful in overcoming the complexities associated with the traditional application building platforms such as the JVM. The APIs can be deployed as substitutes to the complex client codes of the JVM, such as Ruby, because of their user-friendly attributes. There is also the Canvas API that allows developers to draw diagrams in spaces containing solitary graphical elements.

The potential to integrate JavaFX with a variety of web technologies, such as the WebView, fosters compatibility with other language platforms. For example, Java APIs can exchange calls with WebView compliant JavaScript just the same way JavaScript APIs would exchange calls with Java in the WebView environment. Such compatibility features simplify the process of embedding web pages in applications that run on the JavaFX platform.

The JavaFX architecture is designed to integrate multi-touch functionality into graphics applications. Moreover, the Prism functionality of channeling graphics is responsible for accelerating JavaFX operations when deployed alongside a graphics processing unit (GPU). The Prism's flexibility stretches to the ability of determining and selecting alternative graphics platforms whenever the JavaFX-supported GPU features are unavailable. As such, JavaFX is capable of manipulating the functionalities of hardware components to boost the performance and output of its graphics operations.

JavaFX Scene Builder

The JavaFX Scene Builder is one of the self-contained Java solutions that do not require coding. It is further equipped with a visual layout and interactive tools for determining and implementing GUI designs. The JavaFX Scene Builder's user interface layout functionality offers both speed and convenience for integrating graphics such as maps and charts. For example, its drag and drop functionality makes it easier for developers to manipulate the different features and properties. It has a simple structure that favors the application of style sheets and other layout-related aspects of design, thanks to the GUI capabilities of the Cascading Style Sheets (CSS). The analytical tools of the CSS make it easier for Java programmers to predict the impact of its concepts on the overall structure of the JavaFX. The CSS makes it easier for developers to incorporate web pages as embedded features in the JavaFX toolkit. It also simplifies the integration of web applications that are suited for channeling and playing digital files and other forms of multimedia content.

The Scene Builder works with the help of the Java FXML — that is, an editing tool for visual layout. The combination of JavaFX and XML is what gives rise to Java FXML. The FXML coding process involves the integration of markup language features during the development of the JavaFX GUI. A developer can use a Java Scene Builder to transform the FXML into a portable format within an integrated development environment (IDE) for purposes of expanding its operational capabilities. For example, a scene builder can add or expand the logic of an application by simply binding it to the user interface of the FXML file. This is because the FXML operations are fragmented in a way that prevents user interface applications from running at the same time with logic applications.

Although the Java Scene Builder bears default self-contained features, it is readily compatible with various OS platforms including Windows and Linux. It also accommodates different types of IDEs despite being specifically associated with the Netbeans IDE. The preference for Netbeans is attributable to its ability to duplicate the FXML's runtime changes to the Java Scene Builder.

JavaFX versus Java Swing

Prior to the introduction of the JavaFX, Swing was the widely used GUI framework for the Java SE platform. The speculation that JavaFX was destined to replace Swing as the primary client is yet to materialize because both are still relevant and used as viable alternatives alongside other software development toolkits. This shows that anyone interested in learning Java should focus on JavaFX but also direct significant attention towards Swing. There are Java applications that actually use Swing as their primary toolkits in the development of GUI applications. So, what factors would motivate a Java programmer to choose JavaFX over Java Swing, and vice versa? The answer lies in the comparison of the two toolkits. Issues of compatibility, navigation, interactivity, ease of use, and security credential are some of the factors that come into play.

For starters, the two platforms are interoperable, thanks to Swing's flexibility to accommodate JavaFX's advanced features for manipulating graphics and other high-level media properties. But there are more differences relative to the similarities between them. For example, Swing has the JComponent as its primary base for implementing the frame's layout, a situation that rules out the flexibility of additional layouts to sit on top of the component. Additional layouts can only be accommodated upon the creation of new JComponents. This is unlike the JavaFX toolkit which derives its layouts from the node. As such, the layouts simply exist as derived classes of the node parent class to facilitate the extension of functional properties. The result is that the layouts generally inherit properties such as shapes and controls of the nodes, effectively making it easier to expand the composition of layouts.

Although controls are extremely crucial components of GUI application building processes, Swing provides a limited scope of such controls. Developers using Swing mainly interact with buttons, grids, and other basic control parameters. This is unlike JavaFX, which provides a cocktail of wide-ranging control features. These include advanced capabilities for manipulating Pane controls through collapse and organize commands among other adjustments.

The need to deploy animation in GUI implementation would make JavaFX more suitable than Swing. Although Swing is compatible with animations, it does not provide guaranteed paths for deploying the animations. Developers would have to initiate their own launch operations to configure and deploy animation in Swing. In JavaFX, animation is more or less a built-in feature that comes with guaranteed support for style and motion implementations. Therefore, developers do not need to perform preliminary coding preparations for launching animation in Java FX, as is the case with Swing. This convenience is made possible by the ability of nodes to accept the incorporation of animations in functional features such as scene graphs. It makes it easier for developers to perform routine animation procedures and integrate different customizations with ease.

The issue of modernity is equally important when faced with the dilemma of choice between the JavaFX and Swing GUI toolkits. The new device technologies that keep sprouting up every other day require GUI solutions that can keep up with the fast pace of transformations. For example, Swing lacks supports for swipe and touch screen implementation in devices despite these technologies having become common in everyday life. JavaFX, on the other hand, is appropriately equipped with sufficient touch, rotate, and zoom manipulation features as well as other amazing signature tools for swipe and scroll functionalities.

Consistency stands out as one of the most reliable features of the JavaFX toolkit. JavaFX is designed to carefully process events even when they occur in high frequencies. Swing lacks such consistency for processing events. As such, Swing's possession of a higher number of components in comparison to JavaFX does not necessarily translate to greater capabilities when it comes to processing events. The disparities of functionality scopes and capabilities between JavaFX and Swing are also evident in the composition of their development environments. For example, the fast-paced development environment of JavaFX is anchored on scripts and the scene builder. The development environment of Swing absolutely depends on its suite of APIs, a situation that imposes limitations on its speed and efficiency.

Scalability of the composition of components in JavaFX positions it as the better bet for future innovations. The ability to accommodate new and advanced features over time provides greater room for growth and expansion of functionalities for the future. As for Swing, it operates as a complete package that provides little room for expansion of its functionality profile. This is the one difference that would probably inspire a developer to choose JavaFX over Swing. The nature of demands of GUI applications are transformative in nature and a toolkit that can help respond to these transformations is equally important in Java programming.

Java 3D

The latest releases of the Java programming language have been upgraded with advancements that allow developers to integrate three-dimensional (3D) programs in software applications. The Java 3D optimizes performance of development graphic applications in the runtime environment in addition to supporting the delivery of high-quality visual characteristics. The introduction of the Java 3D functionality as an upgrade of Java 2D was occasioned by the need for unique capabilities for capturing and describing object features. It was also meant to provide developers with a wider set of alternatives for implementing OOP concepts in complex application development processes. The Java 3D has the flexibility of working with various types of file formats, making it a suitable option for boosting interactions with runtime loaders during application development processes.

Java 3D operates as an object-oriented API, meaning that it provides support for building graphic software solutions and applets in Java. It has high-level characteristics that allow developers to implement 3D geometry, and to develop the functionalities required to deliver the geometric design. The constructs of the Java 3D API are useful for delivering sufficient data descriptions that allow developers to filter through the infinite number of objects in the virtual worlds. Moreover, developers can write Java 3D API-compatible applets that can have unrestricted access to Java classes and interact freely with the Internet.

The Java 3D API supports interactions for both high-level and low-level constructs for developing graphic applications. The low-level API interactions are largely operations carried out by source codes or frameworks that work to deliver the desired output of graphics design. The high-level APIs, on the other hand, focus on the sophisticated aspects of 3D programming, such as the scene graph, of the Java language. To get a better understanding the 3D API, this chapter provides a further breakdown of its programming philosophy, performance thresholds, application building and applet construction dynamics, object sequence and order, and the operation structure.

Programming Philosophy

The Java 3D API is centered on the OOP guiding philosophy that informs the flexibility to assemble a scene graph from separately constructed graphic objects. According to Sun Microsystems (1999), a scene graph branches out like a tree because the API provides the manipulative abilities for organizing the objects using formatted properties that support access, mutation and node-chaining methods. To achieve this, the 3D API enforces an implementation model for the scene graph, exploits different modes that render program execution, and explores options for scaling the methods for exposing classes.

The scene graph implementation model describes the recommended procedures for rendering or exposing scenes using the Java 3D API. The model simplifies the process by hosting all the aspects of the scene in the form of a universe. This way, developers can access all the details that concern geometric formations, attribute details, and visibility requirements required to deliver a scene. And more importantly, the Java 3D API is designed to enable developers to concentrate on the core aspects of geometry and scene delivery. This is because, unlike the earlier API versions that required developers to perform many ancillary tasks during application development, the 3D version restricts the developers' focus to the primary tasks.

The exploitation of the medium for rendering program executions features the immediate and retained modes as well as the compiled-retained modes, according to the 1999 article by Oracle. These modes actually concern the performance of programs during the implementation of scene graphs. The retained and the compiled-retained modes are known to be more effective performance-wise, thanks to their enhanced scope of rendering applications. For example, the retained mode generates the scene mode construction instructions to be performed by applications, but also describes the particular aspects of the scene that should be transformed by the rendering operation. In addition to the rendering instructions of the retained mode, compiled-retained mode also focuses on breaking down the format of graphs to deliver conclusive scenes. As for the immediate mode, although it lacks the capacity to control combined datasets for rendering operations, it still plays an important role of influencing such operations on object-by-object basis.

Exploration of options for scaling the methods for exposing classes focuses on providing room for other applications and goes beyond Java 3D API's limitations to the mutator and accessor methods. This feature is meant to help developers deploy the API's methods alongside other viable methods that are capable of optimizing performance.

Performance Thresholds

The Java 3D API is a high-performance solution for developing graphic applications. The scope of auxiliary tasks that the API performs lifts weight from the Java programming applications. Whereas this format of task distribution is meant to transfer some data processing responsibilities to the API, it does not in any way compromise on the levels of performance. In fact, this results in optimized output from the API, considering that 3D programming involves high-level abstraction. As such, the complexity and volume of tasks that an API can perform at any one given time keeps changing according to the dynamics of abstraction.

Application Building and Applet Construction Dynamics

The Java code is a useful solution for adding and testing features in the Java 3D programming environment. This goes a long way in determining the level of support that programs can draw from the code. For example, support for external or proprietary modeling applications, such as animation systems, would range from minimal to moderate depending on the levels of formatting compatibility and the variations of geometric designs. The situation is a bit different in the construction of applets because the Java 3D provides significant support for browsers. However, there are occasions when 2D content retains its 2D object format when displayed in 3D browsers, signaling limitations on the levels of support. The limitations of the Java 3D in application building stretches to games. Game developers prefer native applications over non-native applications like Java. But Java 3D is still useful in providing display and performance enhancements in select aspects of game applications. Java's ready portability also enhances its suitability for use in game applications for mobile phones and other small devices.

Object Sequence and Order

Java 3D operations follow a specific order of events that are predefined by object classes. These classes are actually responsible for building and determining the structural composition of the scene graph in addition to dictating the way objects are rendered and viewed. According to Oracle (1999) the *VirtualUniverse* object sits on top of the hierarchy while the *Transform 3D* object sits at the bottom. Some of the other major objects that follow in between the hierarchy according to Oracle (1999) include: "the *Locale*, the *View*, the *PhysicalBody*, the *PhysicalEnvironment*, the *Screen3D*, the *Canvas3D*, and the *SceneGraphObject*." The scene graph object contains the node, the node component, and other types of subsidiary classes (Oracle, 1999).

Chapter Summary

- Developers use GUI toolkits to implement interactive and user-friendly display features in Java programs.

- Swing, JavaFX, and Java 3D are the core segments of GUI toolkits in Java.

- Contrary to perceptions that Swing is obsolete, it is applied as complementary solution alongside the JavaFX.

In the next chapter you will learn about the recommended procedures for handling exceptions in Java.

Chapter Eleven:
Handling of Exceptions

An exception arises when disruptions impair the normal operations of a Java program. Some of the signals of exception may include premature shutdown of a program, inaccessibility of files, or program failure notifications, among others. Network inconsistencies and input of wrong data are some of the common causes of exceptions.

Exception handling in Java provides mechanisms for preventing the collapse of programs during the occurrence of exceptions. The suppression of runtime errors ensures that programs run uninterrupted and execute tasks to completion. This is because exceptions are events that occur at the coding level and it is up to the Java programmer to handle them at the technical level rather than leaving the problem to spill over to the end users. The complex language used to express exceptions when writing codes cannot be understood by end users.

Exception should not be mistaken for errors because, whereas the former can be remedied, the latter leads to complete crashing of the ongoing program activities. Exceptions are displayed as IOException, SQLException, ClassNotFoundException, or RuntimeException among other exception-labeled expressions.

Errors, on the other hand, feature warnings abbreviated as OutOfMemoryError and the like. Therefore, exceptions and errors are separate categories of program disruption agents. The difference between the exceptions and errors is best demonstrated by a flowchart that cascades downwards from the Java program to objects and then throwbacks before branching out to exceptions on one side and errors on the other. The errors arm has its own events under it, while the exceptions arms similarly branches out further as explained below.

Core Exception Categories

There are two core categories of exception — checked and unchecked exceptions. A checked exception is a compiler-generated notification of program disruption. It results from the direct acquisition of the traits of the Throwable class by other classes. Such an exception must be urgently handled within the program by the Java programmer to avoid incurring an error of compilation. The failure to declare a checked exception well in advance risks crippling the coding because it affects the operations of the compiler. The IOException, SQLException, and ClassNotFoundException are all checked exceptions.

The unchecked exception basically acquires the properties of the runtime exception. This means that they are detected later on during runtime operations rather than during compiler operations. In fact, the unchecked exception is simply the RuntimeException in the hierarchy of exceptions, and it must be eliminated using the exception handling tools to maintain the progress of application building operations. The occurrence of a RuntimeException depends on the nature of the operation that is affected. This might be arithmetic, pointer, number format, or indexing operations. For example, the attempted use of a void reference will generate a NullPointerException. Similarly, wrong calculations scuttle runtime operations by imposing the ArithmeticException. The NumberFormatException is a consequence of distorting the recommended procedures for deploying numeric data. IndexOutOfBoundsException occurs when there are attempts to break the barrier for accessing restricted data elements including strings and arrays. It is for this reason that it further branches out to the ArrayIndexOutOfBoundsException and the StringIndexOutOfBoundsException. For example, an ArrayIndexOutOf-BoundsException manifests when there is a mismatch between a value and its destination index.

Keyword Deployment

Exception handling is performed using certain keywords that describe the target operations in a method. The prescribed primary descriptions are expressed in block format and they include *catch*, *finally*, *throw*, *throws*, and *try*. The keywords occur in a predefined hierarchy, with some operating independently and others operating interdependently.

The *try* primary word describes the destination position of the exception code in the method, and it must be accompanied by one other keyword for it to be able to execute the specified instructions. Initialization of the *try* primary keyword should be followed by either the *catch* or the *finally* primary word for the exception handling process to be complete.

A simple trigger of the *catch* word launches the handling of operations in the method, and must be preceded by the *try* keyword. They two keywords are actually used to sandwich the code to protect it. The *catch* block supports declarations of the target exceptions that have been marked for capture. The occurrence of an exception in a code that is under protection already prompts the succeeding *catch* block to initiate the checking of the block that is located right after the *try* parameter. And if the exception is recognizable to the *catch* block, it is captured and conveyed to the *catch* block as a handled event. Catching can process both single and multiple exception handling operations.

The *finally* block keyword triggers the execution of exceptions in the protected code regardless of the outcome of the handling operations of the *catch* block. The non-discriminatory detection capabilities of the *finally* block keyword provides the flexibility for cleaning up the method of exceptions. It helps rid the method of both the handled and unhandled exceptions. The syntax of the outcome of the *finally* block operation resides next to the *catch* block.

This linear sequence of the *try* and *catch* block instructions is usually followed by the *finally* keyword, because each operation has a bearing to the next one, and vice versa. For example, the *try* block essentially maps out the codes that are likely to fall prey to exceptions and exposes them to the *catch* block operation. The operations of the *catch* block, on the other hand, are restricted to the handle exception operations. The *finally* block operation is the actual execution of the target exceptions.

Just as the name suggests, the *throw* keyword signals the invocation of a captured exception. As for the *throws* keyword, despite the near similarity of name to the *throw* keyword, it involves entirely different dynamics. Located at the end of the signature of a method, *throws* is meant for use in exception declarations. Unlike the *throw* exception command that triggers a direct response mechanism, the *throws* command merely signals the presence of a checked exception that was not handled in a particular method. It simply postpones the handling of the checked exceptions. Multiple exception throws are declared using a comma-separated list.

Chapter Summary

- Java programs are prone to operational disruptions that arise from exceptions.

- Exception handling prevents the collapse of programs whenever exceptions occur during the application building processes.

- Keywords are crucial for framing commands and defining exception handing instructions.

In the next chapter you will learn about the management of memory in Java.

Chapter Twelve:
Managing Memory Issues in Java

Responsiveness with regards to the duration it takes for programs to process instructions is one of the key pillars of Java programming. The greater the responsiveness levels, the faster the processing speeds. However, the responsiveness of programs in Java could be derailed by memory leaks. Such memory leaks arise when the redundant objects are stored even when they are no longer useful. This congests the memory and strains the CPU as it struggles to keep pace with unnecessary programs that consume precious resources.

According to Jose F. S. Filho's undated article in *Toptal*, memory leaks may affect performance, resource constraints, the Java heap, and the native memory. Performance-related memory leaks are occasioned by issues such as inefficient garbage collection and overwhelming traffic of objects that get created or deleted. Resource constraint prevails as a result of lack of sufficient memory to accommodate objects. The Java heap leaks concern the heaping of objects in a program due to lack of an outlet mechanism for eliminating unneeded objects. Native memory leaks involve congesting the memory space that is exterior to the Java heap.

The Java memory must work at the optimum level for there to be promptness in the rate of responses to instructions. The availability of an automatic garbage collection feature is meant to prevent memory leaks and optimize the performance of Java programs. But a programmer must always be cautious about the possibilities of the garbage collector getting compromised. This calls for continuous management of garbage collection, and the memory in general, to avoid the painstaking process of detecting and eliminating memory leaks.

Garbage Collection

Garbage collection is the automated process of managing memory in Java. The garbage collection process explores different performance aspects of the heap memory for purposes of detecting active, partially active, and inactive objects within the memory. The garbage collector uses these filters to launch deletion operations for inactive objects in order to free up the memory from unnecessary items. The garbage collector implements the automated memory cleanup process through a two-step process that includes marking and routine deletion.

Marking is the initial phase of identifying the active and inactive components of the memory. It involves scanning to determine the statuses of different objects in the memory. The inactive parts are selected and assigned unique marks to distinguish them from the active or partially active parts. The selective garbage collection procedure ensures that the active objects are not tampered with during the deletion phase. However, the memory scan may consume a lot of time because it is a delicate procedure.

Routine deletion is the process of eliminating inactive objects to leave behind the active ones. The deletion process allows the memory allocator to signal the availability of free space once the unreferenced objects are eliminated. The allocator actually provides automated mechanisms for continuously searching for the availability of free space for allocation. The routine deletion step further provides a compaction-centered deletion alternative for enhancing the performance of the memory. The process simply involves condensation of the referenced objects soon after the deletion of the unreferenced ones to create extra free space.

There are different types of garbage collectors in Java including the serial, the parallel, the G1, and the CMS collectors. The deployment of each of the garbage collection tools depends on the scope of the tasks at hand and the dynamics of application development.

Serial Collector

This particular memory management tool performs garbage collection tasks on a numerical pattern, such that a single virtually-operating processing unit is deployed in the elimination of systematically labeled items. It is suited for both routine and bulky garbage collection events. A combination of marking and compacting procedures facilitates the designation of the aging memory at the head of the heap to give room for the allocation of new memory at the tail end of the heap.

The serial collector's design fits well with applications that operate with minimal pausing or interruption during runtime. This is because a single processing unit is sufficient to support the garbage collection tasks when using this garbage collector. The collector also accommodates high-traffic development environments featuring multiple machines, such as JVMs, running simultaneously. The emergence of IoT has increased the number of embedded devices that operate with low memory thresholds. Such operating environments are suited for the serial garbage collector.

Parallel Collector

The parallel collector, just as its name suggests, works side by side with the default garbage collectors of a program. The use of several threads to execute young generation-powered garbage collection involves the use of the parallel collector. According to Oracle (n.d.), these threads reside in the N garbage collector which comes as a default feature in N CPUs. Its operations are premised on the use of commands to control the garbage collection procedures. However, there are requisite conditions that must prevail for the parallel collector to launch. For example, there must be two or more CPUs for the parallel collector to be able to work alongside the default ones. The default collector, which uses a single thread, is sufficient to perform the required garbage collection operations in a single CPU.

The advantage of the parallel collector working alongside the default ones in multiple CPUs is that it speeds up throughput to minimize the pause durations of the young generation. This makes it useful in bulky operations that are characterized by high frequencies of pause durations. Notably, the scopes of the single-thread operations of the default collector and the multiple-thread operations of the parallel collector stretch to the compacting aspects of the young generation. The compacting process is designed to eliminate gaps that are created between active objects after garbage collection procedures.

CMS Collector

The CMS, or Concurrent Mark Sweep, collector performs garbage collection tasks at the same time with the threads of the application. It is similarly designed to minimize pause durations during garbage collection operations. The CMS also shares the algorithm with the parallel collector, but unlike the parallel collector, the CMS is not tuned to perform compacting procedures on active objects. That is because the CMS performs its operations without necessarily relocating the active objects. It is suited for use in garbage collection environments that permit the sharing of resources with the threads of the application to facilitate concurrent operations.

G1 Collector

The CMS has a successor in the form of the G1 collector. Unveiled with the Java 7 release, the G1 collector combines the features of the parallel and CMS collectors to create versatile garbage collection capabilities. This means it is quite a complex collector and it is discussed in detail in the advanced levels of Java programming.

Generations in Java

Although the marking and routine deletions are widely used to manage the JVM performance, they still pose challenges because of the diversity of objects and their overlapping characteristics. This has necessitated the development of innovative alternatives that provide easier solutions to the memory management issues in Java programming. The segmentation of the heap into smaller units is one such technique that is used to manage the JVM's performance. The smaller units of the heap are known as generations and they include three major segments comprising the young, the old, and the permanent generations. Each of the segments plays predefined roles in the cleanup processes of the heap memory.

Allocation of objects is a continuous process that is accompanied by the aging of the objects. It reaches a point when some of the aged objects become obsolete and cause congestion in the JVM. The young generation segment is specifically designed for the storage of such objects to facilitate minimal levels of automated garbage collection to remove aging objects that are not in use well in advance. This form of minor garbage collection targets completely inactive objects that have short life spans and that can be eliminated expeditiously. The launch of a minor garbage collection operation temporarily halts the operations of all applications until the process is complete.

There are aging objects that escape the young generation's drag net to survive long enough to qualify for automated transfers to the old generation segment. However, these objects will be eliminated at some point through a major garbage collection procedure. Just like a minor garbage collection event, the major garbage collection halts running applications, but it consumes more time because it involves the elimination of active objects, a reality that prompts developers to deploy this option sparingly.

Operations in the permanent generation segment revolve around JVM's descriptions of the classes and methods for deploying applications. This segment houses JVM-generated runtime data that is organized according to class categories. The permanent generation carries a broad portfolio of other data including methods and libraries. But the permanent generation must be cleaned for the JVM to work efficiently. The segment removes classes that are no longer useful through a full garbage collection procedure.

Chapter Summary

- The performance of Java programs can be slowed down by memory leaks or congestion.

- Memory leaks are mainly caused by inefficiency of garbage collection tools.

- Lack of sufficient memory to accommodate objects often occasions resource constraints.

In the next chapter you will learn the dimension of Java programming in the construction of web applications.

Chapter Thirteen:
Java and the Web

The fact that Java hit the scene at a time when the Internet was gradually taking root was a mere coincidence. However, Java has had a symbiotic relationship with the Internet ever since, with each having significant influence in the transformation of the other. For example, Java has been credited for providing secure and portable tools that simplified many aspects of web programming. The widespread use of Java in internet applications, on the other hand, elevated Java into prominence.

Java Web Applications

The symbiotic relationship between Java and the Internet has brought about a variety of web applications that facilitate executions in the web server in addition to supporting the generation of responses to HTTP requests. This chapter explores the role of internet application tools, such as applets and servlets with respect to their relevance in Java programming.

Applets in Java

The Java applet is one of the inventions that sprouted from the search for networked programs for use in the Internet. A Java applet is a little and unique program that is tailored for transmission over the Web. A website has to be compatible with Java to be able to implement an automatic execution of the applet. The applet is packaged as a dynamic, ready-to use, and automatically downloadable program that runs in web browsers. Therefore, all a user needs is to click on a Java applet-configured link to download it and get it running in the browser. The Java applet is one of the characteristics that define the portability of the Java language and its suitability for use in web applications.

The Java applet is useful for exposing server-transmitted data in addition to processing user instructions and accommodating simple operations that are executed within the program's local environment. Deployment of the Java applet more or less transfers the bulk of the tasks it performs from the server side to the client side. However, the applet is vulnerable to cyber attack and other security threats, a reality that has prompted the creation and continuous enhancement of security solutions. For example, the applet's operations are restricted to the Java environment that prevents its exposure to other parts of the computer that might be vulnerable to attacks.

Servlets in Java

The servlet technology is a platform for creating server-side applications for use on the Web. Java programming lends the servlet many features for building powerful applications for the web server. The servlet runs on an API that provides access to a variety of interfaces and options for integrating dynamism in web applications. Developers using the API can deploy these classes and interfaces when building applications for generating servlet HTTP requests and responses as well as implementing generic capabilities. For example, the HttpServlet interface of the API is used to create mechanisms for processing Representations State Transfer (REST) instructions in the HTTP server. The ServletRequest provides the inlet channel, while the ServletResponse provides the outlet channels for the instructions.

The Java servlet significantly addressed the shortcomings that were associated with the server-side programming solutions that were in use prior to its introduction. For example, although the Common Gateway Interface (CGI) facilitated the web server's communication and HTTP interactions with programs in the external environment, it lacked the capacity to accelerate the operations of multiple client processes. Moreover, its design was suited for use with platform-independent programming languages. This limitation made the CGI unsuitable for application development operations that required scalability. The Java servlet introduced platform independence in addition to providing robust capabilities for handling high-traffic multi-client operations. The Java servlet draws its reliable performance attributes from the deployment of threads, rather than processes, when handling requests. The advanced security features of the Java servlet are also crucial for protecting the web server from probable compromise.

Java Web Services

Web services provide standardized, interoperable, and extensible communication portals for different types of applications including client-side and server-side software solutions. The web services are crucial facilitators of interactive tools and frameworks for implementing both simple concepts and complex operations. The availability of XML capabilities in web services is particularly instrumental in the development of machine-readable software applications. The Web Services Description Language (WSDL) forms a crucial part of the descriptive language format. The XML language is also useful in assigning syntax definitions to the different interfaces of web services. In Java programming, web services fall in two major categories that are based on XML and REST technologies.

JAX-WS

The JAX-WS, or Java API for XML Web Services, is pegged on the Standard Object Access Protocol (SOAP) and the XML-based language definitions for implementing a variety of messaging concepts. JAX-WS supports JVM operations thanks to the machine-readable properties of its descriptive language. The design of the SOAP functionality provides messaging properties for enhancing the development of web service applications. The Netbeans IDE is recommended for use in reducing the complexities of deploying the JAX-WS. According to Oracle (2013) the design of the SOAP design must meet certain functionality thresholds that include:

- A formally created contract describing the operational scope of the interfaces hosted within a web service including the messaging and the binding formats. Other than using the JAX-WS portal, contract descriptions can be also implemented using WSDL tools.

- Flexibility to accommodate requisite nonfunctional implementations. The widely referenced recommendations for web services provide guidelines for incorporating the requisite thresholds, along with the suite of vocabulary that is used across the board. This enhances support for a variety of parameters such as security and transaction handling.

- Capabilities to invoke and process asynchronous computing concepts. This requires a standards-hosted infrastructure that facilitates access to messaging protocols, the JAX-WS and a suite of other powerful APIs, and client-side capabilities for invoking asynchronous support.

JAX-RS

JAX-RS, or Java API for RESTful Web Services, supports REST-based implementation of web services. The RESTful properties of the JAX-RS are lightweight and provide user-friendly integration options that are readily compatible with the HTTP. Its design actually favors HTTP interactions rather than the SOAP-driven conventions for web services. As such, unlike the JAX-WS, the JAX-RS is not dependent on the messaging descriptions of the XML.

Project Jersey provides the reference for implementing the JAX-RS in a simplified format that developers can use conveniently when building RESTful web services applications in Java. This platform is equipped with ready-to-use developer tools that eliminate the need for working with many libraries and frameworks for developing applications. Developers also experience greater flexibility when interacting with RESTful interfaces because they are readily compliant with a wide variety of recommended industry standards. These are the reasons behind the cost-effectiveness of the JAX-RS. The Netbeans IDE might be useful in managing the complexities of deploying this particular specification as well. Some of the crucial requirements for deploying the RESTful interface of the JAX-RS include:

- A stateless condition of the web service in use to guarantee interactivity even during interruptions of the server's operations. Such guarantees are necessary for ensuring the recovery of operations in the event of an intended or unintended shutdown of the server.

- Compliant mechanisms for conveying communication between the source and the destination points of instructions. There is always need of understanding between the two points to enhance the flow and execution of instructions.

- Availability of the recommended bandwidth coverage. RESTful applications generally operate in conditions where the bandwidth coverage is limited.

- Ease of use with other related technologies for deploying the Java language in applications.

Chapter Summary

- Java's portable features have always proven useful in the construction of internet applications.

- Web applications provide crucial supports for web server executions in addition to supporting the generation of responses to HTTP requests.

- Java Web Services and Java Web Applications are the main platforms for implementing Java in internet applications.

In the next chapter you will learn about how Java stacks up against other programming languages.

Chapter Fourteen:
Comparing Java to Other Related Languages

Programming languages are the core components in the development, piloting, and implementation of software applications. Different languages come with varying functionality designs, capabilities, limitations, and scopes of deployment. Some of these languages are dynamic and accommodative to shared platforms while others are completely independent due to the nature of their design or complexity of their structures. Java is one of the programming languages that are known to share some degree of similarities with several programming languages including C, C++, C#, and Scala. This chapter looks at the relationship between Java and each of these languages and explores the qualities that set them apart.

Java and the C Language

The C language is one of the earliest programming solutions and its existence dates back to the late-1960s. FORTRAN is one of the few structured programming languages that are known to have existed prior to the advent of the C language. The language has since undergone numerous improvements and has formed the basis of development of other advanced programming languages. The Java language is one such platform that has introduced tools capable of addressing the ever transforming complexities of computing and software development. There are hardly significant similarities between C and Java, except for the resemblance in their syntax. Both are also products of professional software programming engineers.

The major difference between C and Java is that the former is a low-level language while the latter is a high-level language. This means that C provides more of machine-centric coding efficiencies rather than user-centric interpretation conveniences. This makes it difficult for users to deploy and navigate C when building applications. Java, on the other hand, is a high-level language that is equipped with a compiler that supports the interpretation of codes into machine-readable formats. The other difference between the Java and the C language include:

- Java's light-weight ecosystem provides portability across platforms, a feature that is not present in C.

- Java was also designed to overcome the platform dependency limitation that is characteristic of the C language.

- C restricts variable declarations to the beginning of an instruction's block, while Java does not impose limits on the location of variable declarations.

- C language has a structured profile while Java is object-oriented.

Java versus C++

Just like the C language, C++ had been around for a while before Java hit the scene. C++ was one of the native language platforms that dominated computer programming in the years leading to the mid-1990s, because it was tuned for use in a wide variety of applications. It remains relevant to date, thanks to the properties it shares with both Java and C languages. The C++ language is an advancement of the C language, with the main difference being that the former is equipped with class categories. However, unlike the C language, C++ shares some significant similarities with Java. For example, the instructions to execute tasks must be channeled to the main function portals when using Java and C++.

The most conspicuous similarity between Java and C++, however, is that both feature class categories because they are object-oriented languages. These classes simplify troubleshooting procedures in addition to supporting the recycling of codes when using either of the two languages in programming. Both languages feature high-level characteristics for enhancing output and performance. Just like the Java language, the C++ language is equipped with general purpose credentials for implementing both simple and complex computing concepts. This means that both Java and C++ are suited for use in a variety of desktop applications and OS platforms as well as IoT innovations. Both languages accommodate the use of primitive data types in code compilation processes.

The Java and C++ languages expose developers to wide varieties of tools — such as client libraries, source codes, and frameworks — that accelerate the processes of building applications. Java and C++ share syntax characteristics, meaning that some aspects of their syntax coding are identical. Java and C++ also share similarities in the use of loops in instruction coding. A loop instruction like 'else' would appear in the same format in both Java and C++. The same applies to the widely used conditional statements, such as if-else, in the two programming languages. Developers Java and C++ encounter similar operators for performing arithmetic operations or functions.

A look at the differences between the two programming languages shows that Java is fast and more convenient to write than C++. This is because it only requires a couple of lines to code Java. Moreover, C++ is quite bulky compared to Java because the latter's lightweight programs feature fewer counts of classes, methods, and other operational parameters. The C++ platform tends to pack these program parameters in large-scale proportions. Unlike Java, C++ conveniently performs low-level operations despite its high-level functionality features. That means the C++ language has unique level compatibilities that are well suited for systems programming compared to the Java language which is biased towards application programming. This is because C++ has more proximity to hardware platforms than Java by virtue of its flexibility for interacting with low-level applications. Whereas Java provides cross-platform operational capabilities, C++ provides a single platform as a native application. This makes Java compatible with any platform that houses the JVM, unlike the C++ which would require a code to be written afresh for it to adjust to changes in the platforms that are in use. The other major differences between Java and C++ include:

- The C++ language lacks the system controlled memory management mechanism of Java, making it more vulnerable to memory setbacks compared to Java.

- The Java language has both compilation and interpretation attributes, while C++ has only the compilation attribute.

- Java has built-in multithreading capabilities that facilitate multi-tasking, while C++ does not. This makes Java a more suitable option than C++ for handling high volumes of data traffic during application development.

- Although both C++ and Java are object-oriented languages that support inheritance, Java does not provide the flexibility of accommodating multiple inheritance processes like C++.

- Whereas C++ bears the infrastructure for supporting the goto statements, pointers, and operator overloading, Java does not provide support for any of these variables.

- The support for documentation comments that is inherent in Java is not available in C++.

- Unlike the C++ language, Java lacks a virtual keyword support feature.

Java versus C#

C# is a Microsoft-developed programming language that provides modernized solutions for developing software applications. Released in 2005, the C# language joined the list of emerging programming languages that were created by elite engineers in leading technology companies. Anders Hejlsberg is credited for having successfully led the Microsoft team of engineers that developed the C# language. The C# language shares several similarities with Java including their general-purpose functionalities, modernization attributes, and object-oriented design.

However, the two languages are significantly different from each other in terms of structure, operations, and architecture. For example, whereas operator overloading is a nonexistent feature in Java, it is one of the highlight features in C#. The two languages also operate on different runtime environments since C# uses the Common Language Runtime (CLR) as opposed to Java's JVM. Unlike the Java API, which operates as an open-source community-controlled software development solution, the C# API restricts developers to the Microsoft programming tools. In fact, C# only works with the Windows OS and is yet to be transformed into a global programming language for use with other OS platforms. The other differences between Java and C# include:

- Java does not possess task-delegation capabilities like the C# language.

- Whereas the Java accommodates only a single public class within its source code at a time, the C# language accommodates several public classes within its source codes.

- The goto statement is a supported feature in C# while it is an incompatible feature in Java.

- Java's check and uncheck functionalities for exception handling are not available in C#. The absence of these features in the C# is a setback because they are useful for managing operational inconsistencies in programming.

- C# is useful in programming processes requiring conditional compiling. Java does not provide support for conditional compiling.

- Whereas structures and unions are built-in features in C#, they are not available in Java.

Java versus Scala

Scala is an object-oriented programming language that has been in existence since its release in 2003. It was largely developed on the foundation principles of the Java language. For example, just like the Java language, the Scala language uses the JVM to perform programming operations. This makes Scala compatible with Java's libraries and developer tools. Such compatibilities allow developers to reuse Java codes when in need of shifting to the Scala language when building applications. In fact, Java and Scala can be used interchangeably to perform calls to each other. Scala also shares several IDEs with Java including Netbeans, making it easier for developers to manage complex application development procedures.

But there are aspects of Scala's functionality properties that make it different from the Java language. Scala's paradigmatic orientation actually stretches beyond object-oriented programming because it provides the infrastructure for functional programming. This is the particular area where Scala is considered to provide additional programming features compared to Java. This means that developers can access the function passing feature when using Scala as opposed to Java. Developers seeking for a lighter programming solution than Java will find that solution in Scala. This is because the codes in Scala are built using the type inference feature that creates shorter lines compared to Java. The other major differences between Java and Scala include:

- Java is easier to learn than Scala because the minimal coding operations in the latter make it less predictable. Java's immense coding operations are actually more predictable and grant users greater control over an application.

- Unlike Java, Scala's overall design is meant for straight-forward expression of the programming layout.

- Java and Scala use different syntax formats, with the one for Java possessing friendlier layout and appearance.

- Scala's operator overloading functionality is not available in Java, making the former more flexible to creating a variety of operators compared to the latter. However, it is important to remember that Java supports other types of overloading including constructor overloading and method overloading.

Chapter Summary

- Java shares significant similarities with several programming languages including C, C++, C#, and Scala.

- A common similarity between Java and other modern programming languages is that they were created by professional engineers in leading IT companies.

Final Words

This book has provided you with helpful insights into the basic aspects of Java programming. However, Java is a very wide area of study and a single book cannot be sufficient to cover all the areas about this particular subject. Once you familiarize yourself with the basic concepts of Java programming, you need to expand your knowledge by exploring the programming language at the intermediate and advanced levels. Therefore, the chapters in this book have been designed to prepare you for the more involving and adventurous implementation of Java programming. This book will always remain your important reference companion even as you progress to the intermediate and advanced levels of the programming language.

Made in the USA
Las Vegas, NV
22 September 2023